Live Well: My Ukrainian Upbringing

and Other Stories

Live Well: My Ukrainian Upbringing
and Other Stories

Marion Mutala

Back Cover Photographs

St. John the Evangelist Ukrainian Catholic Church located in the village of Prud'homme Saskatchewan was constructed in 1945. The author's relatives Peter and Mary (Dubyk)Hryniuk, were one of the original founding members and their family continue to lovingly care for this church.

Hryniuk family barn located in the Prud'homme district of Saskatchewan. This barn is symbolic of the many red barns found in Western Saskatchewan farms and is about 90 years old. It was newly renovated in 2020 and is significant as it is owned by a cousin to my mother Sophie (Dubyk) Mutala and myself.

Cover Art

The cover artwork was the creation of stained glass artist Rodney Ketsa, who lived in Smoky Lake at the time. He was commissioned to do the artwork. The monument was designed and built by the Vegreville Branch of the Alberta Ukrainian Canadian Congress - Alberta Provincial Council, in 1991.

It was dedicated on the occasion of the centenary of Ukrainian settlement in Alberta, (1891-1991/1892-1992). On the bronze plaque which stands beside the monument, it states: "In tribute to all pioneers who settled and through hard work and determination created a lasting legacy for all."

See more info at:
https://issuu.com/thenewsadvertiser/docs/vna_june_03___2020_-_web/s/10608208

First Edition

Hidden Brook Press
www.HiddenBrookPress.com
writers@HiddenBrookPress.com

Copyright © 2021 Hidden Brook Press
Copyright © 2021 Marion Mutala

All rights for story and characters revert to the author. All rights for book, layout and design remain with Hidden Brook Press. No part of this book may be reproduced except by a reviewer who may quote brief passages in a review. The use of any part of this publication reproduced, transmitted in any form or by any means, electronic, mechanical, photocopied, recorded or otherwise stored in a retrieval system without prior written consent of the publisher is an infringement of the copyright law.

This book is a work of fiction. Names, characters, places and events are either products of the author's imagination or are employed fictitiously. Any resemblance to actual events, locales or persons, living or dead, is entirely coincidental.

Title – Live Well: My Ukrainian Upbringing
         and Other Stories
Author – Marion Mutala

Editor – Richard M. Grove
Front Cover Art – Rodney Ketsa
Back Cover Photos – Martin Hryniuk
Cover Design – Richard M. Grove
Layout and Design – Richard M. Grove

Typeset in Garamond
Printed and bound in Canada
Distributed in USA by Ingram,
        in Canada by Hidden Brook Distribution

Library and Archives Canada Cataloguing in Publication

Title: Live well : my Ukrainian upbringing and other stories / Marion Mutala.
Names: Mutala, Marion, 1957- author.
Identifiers: Canadiana 20210181974 | ISBN 9781989786352 (softcover)
Subjects: LCSH: Mutala, Marion, 1957- —Anecdotes. |
        CSH: Ukrainian Canadians—Saskatchewan—Anecdotes. |
LCSH: Saskatchewan—Biography—Anecdotes. | LCGFT: Anecdotes.
Classification: LCC FC3550.U5 Z7 2021 |
        DDC 971.24/004917910092—dc23

To My
Three Adult Children:
My Son Symret
and
Partner Shylah
and
My Daughter Natasha
and
Her Partner Robert,
and my son
Jacob-Joshua

Table of Contents

1 – Baba's Trunk – *p. 1*

2 – Exercising My Rights – *p. 14*

3 – Sophie and August: A Love Story – *p. 16*

4 – Creamy, White Gold – *p. 28*

5 – Mud Pies – *p. 32*

6 – Turkey Torment – *p. 36*

7 – 50 Loads of Hay – *p. 38*

8 – My Place, My Pillow – *p. 42*

9 – The Great Pyrohy Eat Off – *p. 45*

10 – Connected – *p. 51*

11 – Chasing the Divine – *p. 54*

12 – What History Teaches Us About Soil – *p. 57*

13 – The Five F's

    1 – The Gift of Faith – *p. 61*

    2 – The Second "F" – *p. 62*

    3 – Baba's Borsch – *p. 66*

    4 – Friends and Fun – *p. 68*

14 – The Blizzard – *p. 71*

15 – Wild Horses at Robinson Bay – *p. 73*

16 – Do I Finally Have Your Attention? – *p. 77*

17 – Rant and Radical, Part of My Family Heritage – *p. 79*

18 – Boona/Boon – *p. 82*

19 – Escape – *p. 87*

20 – The Obsession – *p. 104*

21 – But Diamonds Are a Girl's Best Friend – *p. 108*

22 – Hanky Panky – *p. 111*

23 – He's Hot – *p. 114*

24 – One Simple Glance – *p. 116*

25 – BFF – *p. 121*

26 – Secrets – *p. 124*

27 – 666-Conn – *p. 129*

28 – Wrangled – *p. 134*

29 – The Deep Sleep – *p. 139*

30 – Two Point Five Hours – *p. 142*

31 – Live Well – *p. 147*

32 – Constant Craving in the Year of COVID-19 – *p. 152*

About the Author – *p. 156*

Baba's Trunk

It was huge. So heavy, it took two strong men to pull it. One person could not lift it. It contained everything she owned. Life savings, food, clothes, passports, garden seeds, tools, religious artifacts like an icon and the precious family Bible, a gold-plated crucifix, and a rosary. All her worldly precious possessions were contained in that trunk. She had even packed a gigantic flat rock to make kapusta, (sauerkraut) in a wooden barrel. After all, who knew what this new country would have? She had a one-way ticket and very little chance of ever returning home to Ukraine.

Beautiful Icon of Mary and Jesus.

This was Baba's trunk. All she owned was packed into this brown, wooden, metal-hinged, steamer trunk – older than dirt – with leather strapped around the trunk's middle and fastened with buckles to hold it in place. Stuffed and packed to the brim. That trunk contained her entire belongings. Such trunks were the source of existence to the early Ukrainian settlers immigrating to kah-nah-da from what was often referred to as the "old country," some far-off land. Who knew what hell lived on the other side of the world?

Like other Ukrainian immigrants, my grandparents had set out from the villages by wagon to catch a train that would take them to a larger centre in Germany for their passage to paradise. Their goodbyes would have been said in the villages, the tears final. Ukrainians came to Canada in droves during the first wave of immigration from 1891-1914. Ukraine was in a constant state of turmoil, with soldiers fighting against invading countries since Ukraine was part of the Austro-Hungarian Empire at the start of the First World War in 1914.

Red River Cart and Oxen.

The Galicia area was one of the poorest and most over-populated regions of Ukraine at this time and had experienced blights and famines. Posters in Europe advertised that Canada was "the land of milk and honey," where immigrants would find bigger, better opportunities like the chance to own and farm their own land. Another huge attraction was that they would have political and religious freedom in Canada.

Beaded Sheepskin Vest.

The steamship trip lasted about 18 days. Forget about cruise cabin: some ships were hastily converted cargo ships; sometimes the Canadian Pacific Railway even carried passengers in their cattle boats. The travellers on board suffered greatly from poor ventilation and crawling insects. Many slept with the animals on the bottom of the ship, puking their guts out from seasickness. The stench and filth would have been gut-wrenching. They had to be made of tough stuff to survive, otherwise they would end up dying on the ship and being thrown overboard. There was no place on the boat to keep bodies. While many of these hopeful immigrants died from illness or childbirth and did not survive the voyage, that was not my grandparents' fate. It is amazing just how many Ukrainians did make it to Canada during that first wave of immigration.

Dr. Joseph Oleskiw, an agriculturist from Galicia, had visited western Canada and personally confirmed that the Canadian prairies were suitable for Ukrainian farmers. In 1895, he published two pamphlets, "On Free Lands" and "On Emigration," stating that 160 acres (64 hectares) of land were available in Canada for a nominal $10 registration fee. However, 10 dollars might be a pittance now but then one had to work half a year to save that amount and it was backbreaking work clearing land or any job whether done by male or female. Most needed work was done by hand and labour-intensive and often involved working 10-hour days.

More than 170,000 Ukrainians arrived in Canada between 1891 and 1914, an influx that had a tremendous impact on the population of the prairie region. It cost $150 per person for boat and train passage fees. Immigrants had to sell off all their land and belongings to afford the passage to come. They often had little or no money when they arrived.

This story is focused on the tale of one Ukrainian immigrant family: my grandparents, Baba Tessie Woznakowski from Zupkova, Sokal region and Dido Stefan Dubyk from Perespa, Sokal region neighbouring villages about five kilometres apart. It is unknown whether my grandparents were childhood sweethearts or that they even knew each other before they arrived in Canada.

Tessie was born in 1890; she immigrated to Canada in 1912 with her cousin, John Nowosad, and settled in Saskatoon, Saskatchewan. Stefan was born in 1888; in 1911, he came to Canada by boat, docking in Quebec City, and then took the train to Winnipeg. There, he was detained in an 'immigration home' by immigration officials who, after 1895, made the decisions about where new immigrants could settle. Stefan then travelled by prairie cart to Saskatoon.

On arrival, both Tessie and Stefan worked at the King George Hotel together, so perhaps that is where their love story began. The owners of the King George Hotel went bankrupt and did not pay the employees, so the workers took silverware, pots and pans in payment for their work. They worked as maintenance or labourers at the hotel.

They married in 1913 and moved to Krydor, where they both worked as farm labourers: Stefan for Martin Borycki and Tessie for the Diditch family. Tessie did both inside and outside work: families would often hire a girl to help with gardening, cooking, cleaning, and taking care of children, especially when women had a new baby.

My Grandparent's Stefan Dubyk and Tessie Woznakowski who came to Canada in 1911 and 1912 from Western Ukraine.

The work was very hard as they were required to chop trees to clear the land with a biga (a type of pick with one wide side and the other side shaped like an axe). The going wage during that period was between 10 and 25 cents per hour. Many people worked long hours every day. Sometimes food and lodging were included especially if they could not get workers, but one had to negotiate and at times that was taken off their wages. The value of board for males was $16.40 per month and for females $13.96. per month.

In August 1914, their first daughter, Millie, was born. In April 1916, they moved to their homestead, a quarter section of land about five kilometres north and six kilometres east of Mayfair, three kilometres south of Ringleton Firs. Stefan received the patent (or title) for this section in March 1921. But this land was very poor land for farming and quite rocky. Their temporary house was called a buda and was dug out in the ground. The roof was covered with plowed sod furrows.

This is where they were living when Stefan's brother, Wasyl (Bill), who immigrated to Canada in 1926, came to visit them. Bill remarked to family members that when he first visited his brother and wife, they were living in a mud house in the side of the hill, despite having lived in Canada for 14 years. Stefan and Bill were the only Dubyk immediate family members who immigrated to Canada.

Their farming began by clearing the quarter of land with one horse named Passa and one steer. Tessie had to lead the animals around by their halter. She said that often, when the horse and the steer were hitched to the mower together, the steer, desperate to keep flies and mosquitoes away, would become stubborn and run into the nearby slough, mower and all. Smoke from fire was the only means of protecting animals from the incessant bugs.

Stefan hauled logs from the logging camp, and with Tessie's help, their home was built. The roof was made from long hay cut with a scythe from a slough, then tied into sheaves. This hay was placed on a wooden frame. Tessie mud-plastered the logs and white-washed the inside and outside of their homes by hand. The mud-plaster floor was swept with a broom made of fine willows tied with twine. Our grandparents were industrious and emulated the farming and building techniques they had used in Ukraine. Physically hard work was needed daily just to survive.

Tessie and Stefan would often get up at four o'clock in the morning and travel 40 kilometres to Hafford by horse and buggy for supplies. They milked cows and shipped cream in cream cans by train to Shellbrook, Saskatchewan for some cash, which was vital to their survival.

Baba and Dido lived on this homestead for 12 years; six of their seven children were born there. When the Dubyk children started school at Ringleton Firs, it was a real hardship because of the poor roads, deep snow and cold winter weather. The children had many chores to do each day before school, like chopping wood to keep the house warm or getting water.

The crops grew tall, but sometimes unexpected frost or a drought occurred before they could be harvested. Gardens froze too, so food was always scarce, and they often went hungry. When the cow's milk dried up, there was no milk to drink. Tea was a cheap staple and, on occasion, was all there was to fight off hunger: Tessie always had a pot of tea sitting on her wood and coal stove.

Pedahay (also called varenyky or perogies) were Ukrainian staples made from dough and potatoes, and often kept them from starving. Plum perogies were made on special occasions when they had fruit. Baba also baked bread and made kapusta, (sauerkraut), from cabbage, salt and boiled water, and placed it in a wooden barrel to sour, putting to good use the big, flat rock from back home. Research now shows that cabbage, garlic and onions — foods that Ukrainians ate in abundance — are very healthy for you as they have strong medicinal qualities.

Plum stuffed Varenyky.

Tessie became efficient at treating others with her first aid medicines using herbs and boiling willow roots for salve, and picking berries, leaves and plants to use as specialty teas and for medicinal drinks. Hot rocks steamed with water were used to get rid of colds; mustard plasters were made with flour and dry mustard, put on flannel cloths, and placed on a sick person's chest as a home remedy to ward off coughs and pneumonia. Garlic and goose fat were also medicinal ingredients used to heal. Today, she might be called a Babka-Sheptukha, a Ukrainian folk healer (sometimes called a "granny whisperer"). It was a matter of survival and Tessie was a smart woman and a fast learner.

In their buggy, Tessie and Stefan would go fishing in the summer at Meeting Lake. The fish they caught were cleaned and salted with onions (if available), put into wooden pails, and buried in the ground to stay cold. Burying things deep in the ground prevented food from spoiling. This acted as their refrigerator. Later, when they had dug a well, produce was hung in pails and placed near the cold water to keep cool. When they had milk, they made cottage cheese, which was salted and stored in the ground as well.

During summer, when the slough grass was thick and green, the grass was cut and put into gunny sacks to make mattresses for the family to sleep on. Tessie would also make thick, feather quilts to keep everyone warm in the winter, since ice often formed in the reservoir of the stoves and on the bottom of doors and windows, as well as on the roof and ceiling inside their home. When the snow melted in the springtime, it would rain indoors as well.

In winter, huge holes were cut in the ice so that the family and cattle would have water to drink. Outdoor toilets were always a challenge. Since going to the outhouse when it was cold and dark was not a pleasant experience, an empty gas can was often used at night (or in winter), to go to the bathroom, then emptied outside once a day.

Finally, after 16 years of hardship, trying to make ends meet with six children, Baba and Dido could afford to buy land at Hafford. Today, Hafford could be considered the Ukrainian capital of Saskatchewan. Even today its street signs are in Ukrainian, which uses the Cyrillic alphabet. Canada is now the third-largest country with Ukrainian-speaking immigrants with most of them living in the Prairie Provinces.

In 1928, the Dubyks moved three kilometres west and six kilometres north of Hafford to one quarter of purchased land. The family believes that this land was likely bought from the Canadian Pacific Railway and that it was chosen because there

A painting by Gonda in 1985
My Grandparent's Stefan Dubyk and Tessie (Woznakowski) Dubyk
Second Homestead moved there in 1928 and still standing
3 kilometres west and six kilometers north of Hafford, Saskatchewan.

were fewer trees, and it would perhaps be easier to farm. However, this land was not yet broken and still had a lot of stones to clear. Labour for stone-picking was often provided by the children: even the little ones were expected to pitch in and help.

Clearing the land proved to be a slow, back-breaking job. Moreover, until they finished building their new home, the Dubyk family lived in a granary on that land. A granary is where farmers store their grain before they take it to market to sell.

In fact, their youngest daughter, Anne, was delivered by Dr. Arthur Rose and Nurse Rose Bedier in this granary not long after the Dubyks moved there. Imagine delivering a baby in such surroundings! The new home was built of logs and was shingled with sod, a mixture of grass and mud. Tessie always plastered and white-washed her homes; without the whitewash, when the rain came, the plaster would fall off.

By 1930, the Great Depression and drought were taking a toll on the family. Tessie would make 12 loaves of bread at one time in her outdoor clay oven, called a piche, to feed her growing family. Bread and tea might be all they had at times during the Depression as there was a food shortage.

The 1937 harvest brought only three-quarters of a wagon box of wheat. The wheat quality was pathetic and contained a lot of pigweed seeds in it. The family of nine went on government relief, which provided the entire family with only $8 a month. They also received a big, round cheese and salted cod that came by train from down east.

Other years, when the crops were better, the wagonload of wheat was hauled to Radisson, 41 kilometres away. They exchanged the hauled wheat for flour, which provided many valuable meals. The flour sacks were sewn into dresses, sheets, pillowcases, and tea towels. Nothing was wasted and everything was reused or recycled. Both are important and clothes that children naturally grew out of were passed done to be worn by another child but if it did not fit, they could take the material apart and remake or recycle it to fit.

Tessie's laundry was all done by hand in tubs with a washboard. Soap was made by hand from lye and pig fat. In the winter, washed clothes were hung outside until they were frozen dry and then brought in and hung around the stove. Her hands were often red and sore from all the washing.

During the good years, Tessie made homebrew called horilka. Potatoes, raisins, wheat, yeast, sugar and bran were fermented by the woodstove, then distilled and enjoyed like a shooter. A shooter is when you drink a small amount of alcohol in a shot glass down the hatch at once. It was a very potent drink.

The Dubyk family always created their own fun and loved to play cards games: 31 (also called Rap-up), and Kaiser were family favourites. They also were a musical family and, in later years, were able to purchase a fiddle, drums, accordion, banjo, and saxophone. They formed an orchestra that played at weddings and parties in the area. They were sometimes paid for their music.

In August 1944, Stefan died of throat cancer at the young age of 56. Tessie and her son, Peter, continued to farm. Peter helped to build a home in Hafford with some modern conveniences like running water, indoor toilet, electrical power, and a

My Grandparent's Stefan Dubyk and Tessie (Woznakowski) Dubyk buried at Hafford, Saskatchewan and their 7 children listed on the back of their headstone. My mom was Sophie (Dubyk) Mutala (1918-2007).

wringer washer. Tessie died of heart failure in 1962 at the age of 72. She is buried in the Hafford Cemetery beside Stefan.

Baba and Dido arrived to a harsh life in Saskatchewan, and survived without roads, running water, electricity and sometimes even without food. They lived through two world wars and the Great Depression. Today, 13.5 per cent of Saskatchewan residents are of Ukrainian ancestry. Working as farmers, cooks, domestic workers, labourers, healers, teachers, nurses, politicians and more, our ancestors contributed to the great province of Saskatchewan. They would be proud to know that the former Premier Brad Wall honoured and recognized our Ukrainian ancestors for their significant contributions to Saskatchewan by declaring 2016 the Year of Saskatchewan Ukrainians.

Baba's trunk travelled across the ocean with her. It carried all that she owned, bridging her old life with the new. Like many other trunks brought by many other immigrants, that trunk, which my sister still has was precious.

An old trunk.

Exercising My Rights

(*Women's right to vote began in the three prairie provinces in 1916, suffrage was given to women in Manitoba, Saskatchewan and Alberta. Saskatchewan women got the right to vote on March 14, 1916. The Liberals, Farmer Labour Group was the official opposition during the 1920's. This party later became the Co-operative Commonwealth Federation or CCF. Tommy Douglas was the premier of Saskatchewan and responsible for setting up Medicare in Canada. He was a social-democrat and became the leader of the democratic socialist party in Canada which became the provincial government in 1944. The other party was the United Farmers Independent Labour Party. This story occurs in the 1940's.)*

"Who are you voting for?" my husband said. "None of your business, it's a secret ballot."

"Well, you have to vote for the same person as me." he declared.

"No, I do not," I said firmly.

"Yes, you do, or you will cancel out my vote?"

"I get to vote for whomever I want." I said gratefully. "This is a free country – Canada, I'm a naturalized citizen and as a woman I finally have my own vote and it counts the same as yours."

"Well," her husband murmured loudly, "if you do not vote for the same party as me, I'm not taking you to town to vote."

"Well then, don't," I replied strongly. "But I will vote anyway, even if I must walk from the farm all the way to town to exercise my vote. I've walked 10 kilometres before and I can do it again just to make sure my voice is heard in this election.

Everyone will see me walking and wonder why I'm walking, rather than riding with you. Then, you will be terribly embarrassed and full of shame. So, you do whatever you want," I exclaimed rather loudly as I stomped out of the room.

We rode side by side silently, in the horse and buggy, all the way to town and back to vote.

A few years later, my cousin told me she heard via the grapevine that they had voted for the same party, the Co-operative Commonwealth Federation or CCF which eventually gave Canadians free Medicare.

(True story as told to me by my cousin about her parents who immigrated in 1926. As new immigrants to Canada this was her mother's first voting experience ever and the first time in Saskatchewan.)

Old Wagon Wheels.

Sophie and August: A Love Story

Sophie's preparation

Sophie was born near Hafford, Saskatchewan about 80 kilometres north from Saskatoon. She was born on September 23, 1918, the third child of Tessie Woznakowski and Stefan Dubyk. She completed her schooling up to grade six as there were no schools in this area to continue her education. She wished there were opportunities to further her learning. Sophie loved school and remembers receiving a dress and hat as first prize from her teacher for doing so well. She loved to read and dream, like any young girl, especially about getting married to a royal prince. However, because of the second world war there was a shortage of available men in Saskatchewan.

Good training

Sophie wanted to marry and have a family. As a youngster, she had helped bake bread, make perogies, wash the clothes on the washboard, cut the wood with her brother, using a double handled saw, fill mattresses with clean hay to sleep on and make feather quilts. By the age of 14, Sophie was working for various families in the area, learning to make beautiful, fluffy buttermilk pancakes, flaky pie crusts, bread, doughnuts and how to grow a bountiful garden. All this experience would be put to good use later, when Sophie became a wife and mother and had to feed her own family of 10 children, me being number nine of the 10. All she needed was to find a husband: no easy task when you are isolated on the farm with no real means of transportation and no eligible bachelors around.

An arranged marriage

In September 1940, August Mutala was in Hobel's store in the small village of 200 people of Kenaston, Saskatchewan, 80 kilometres south of Saskatoon. He was visiting with Mary and Jacob Dubyk who ran the store at that time. Jacob was a cousin to Sophie's dad, Stefan.

Mary asked August if he was married and when he replied, "No." Mary said, "I have just the girl for you, but you must be religious." August was 35 years of age and not getting any younger; he said he could be religious. So, Mary wrote to Sophie and two weeks later, August travelled by train 147 kilometres to Radisson to meet Sophie and her family. Her parents lived in a one- bedroom house and since there was no privacy, Sophie and August went and talked in the bedroom. What did they talk about? One can only surmise. In those days, Sophie knew that at 22 years of age she was considered a spinster and that the pickings were slim.

The surprise visit

Sophie was a smart woman who knew that before she would agree to marriage, it was important to check out her future home. So, she went on a surprise trek all the way from Hafford to the Hanley/Kenaston area, 147 kilometres. Her brother, Alex, as chaperone, drove her in his Overland car, a touring car, similar to the Model T Ford which featured a two-cylinder water-cooled engine that was mounted up front under the hood. The car also featured a removable switch plug so that it could not be driven if it were removed. It was worth about $500.00 brand new, but of course, this was a second-hand vehicle.

Off Sophie went on quite a journey to meet her future husband and to visit the farm. It was a real surprise visit since August was not home, but out somewhere working in the fields. Sophie saw the house, the farmyard, and barn and recognized that August was no slouch.

The house was a mansion compared to the one she had grown up in: it had a porch, milk room, large kitchen, living room and three bedrooms (one on the main floor and two on the upper level), and the farmyard had a barn, granaries, an old well and a huge garden space. It was enormous compared to the one-bedroom home inhabited by the nine people in her family. August came for one last visit to her parents' home and that time, he asked Sophie's dad, for permission to marry her. Sophie had the option to say no, but as she told her daughter many years later, she thought August was handsome.

Two meetings

So, after meeting only twice, the wedding was planned for November 2, 1940 in the Ukrainian Catholic Church in Hafford. Ukrainian weddings were usually three-day affairs. Preparations included a lot of fun, frivolity and a mock wedding. In a small village, there were three phases to a Ukrainian wedding, the pre-wedding, the wedding phase and the post wedding phase. Most weddings took place immediately after harvest, not in November. However, as both Sophie and August did not want to spend another winter alone (remember they were not getting any younger), they decided to get married soon. Perhaps this is where the expression, "Why wait for spring, do it now?" originated.

As part of the preparation for the wedding, August lovingly purchased Sophie's wedding gown a white dress and a bouquet of flowers, shoes and veil to wear that day. Sophie, in return, bought him a white shirt and tie because August already owned a good black suit. To gift each other these special wedding purchases shows their love and commitment to each other.

The wedding day

It was a cold, snowy day in November and of course they got stuck in the snow going to the church. This did not prevent them from getting to the church on time at 10 am, since weddings occurred on Sunday mornings. Like any Ukrainian wedding, the ceremony was about two hours long, with much chanting and singing at church. Sophie's family was present, but August had no family to attend since he had emigrated from

Slovakia. This would have been a happy occasion. Ukrainians love a good party, especially a wedding celebration, and the couple was pleased to get married.

3 Loaves of Kolach bread symbolizing the Holy Trinity used for Ukrainian Christmas Eve Supper.

An Example of Wedding Bread with Doves called Korovai often used at Ukrainian weddings. This Korovai bread was made by Mary Kalist for my book I wrote about Ukrainian Weddings called:
Baba's Babushka: A Magical Ukrainian Wedding.

The ceremony

In 1940, Ukrainians usually married within their own cultural group. Father Duhromoratsky performed the wedding ceremony, he asked Sophie, "Aren't there any good Ukrainian men left?" Had Father done his homework, he would have known there were very few available men of any nationality left! August emigrated from Czechoslovakia: he was of Slovak descent with no family here. August gave the priest $15 for performing the ceremony. This was a lot of money as the average daily wage was 30 cents per hour, which today, would equate to $5.51 per hour. Then Father Duhromoratsky praised the Slovaks.

My Parents August Mutala and Sophie (Dubyk) Mutala on their Wedding day November 2nd, 1940 at Hafford, Saskatchewan.

The feast

The wedding reception was held at the Dubyk farm. Can you imagine, 50 people celebrating in that tiny, one-bedroom house? Supper consisted of roast pork, potatoes, vegetables, holubtsi (cabbage rolls), and breads. Cakes were supplied by the neighbour ladies. Perogies were not served at the wedding meal, as they were considered ordinary, common food – my how times have changed! A recent survey in Canada said perogies were the number one favourite food in Western Canada.

There was lots of food, family, friends, fun, music and drink of course. Many toasts were given while guests sang the blessing song *Na mnohe lyeetah*, which translates to May God Grant You Many, Many Years Together.

Cabbage Rolls made with rice or Holubtsi considered a delicacy.

The dance

Ukrainian weddings usually took place over three days but since Sophie and August were married in wintertime, this was impossible. The family and friends partied and stayed up all night- after all, there were no rooms to sleep in. Sophie's brothers and sisters were very musical and along with a neighbour, John Gall, provided the music.

The band members that accompanied John were Sophie's sister, Ann on accordion, her brother Bill on saxophone, her brother Nick on violin, her brother Alex on drums and her brother Peter on banjo. The Dubyks played for many weddings. They sounded so good and had great fun singing, joking and of course, drinking lots of horilka. During Ukrainian weddings, homebrew was served in teapots in case of a Royal Canadian Mounted Police (R.C.M.P.) raid. Since homebrew was illegal, they wrapped jugs of it to look like presents. That evening, they ran out of booze and Sophie's brothers had to make a "booze run" to the neighbours: they got stuck in the snow on the way back and did not return to the wedding that night.

My Mother Sophie's Sister Ann Novokowski on Accordion and her Three Brothers, Peter Dubyk on violin, Bill Dubyk on drums and Nick Dubyk on banjo. They were known as The Dubyk Band.

The wedding night

In the morning, Sophie's brother Bill drove the newlyweds to catch the train in Radisson to Hanley, where Coral Trask's father gave them a ride to the farm for $2 which seemed a lot considering gas was 18 cents a gallon. The wedding night was delayed till they reached their new home together on the farm near Kenaston. Sophie's sister, Millie, packed the happy couple a lunch for the train ride—and sent along a plate of chicken bones in a bag for a joke. Such prankster tricks were a natural part of Ukrainian culture.

The wedding gifts

On January 6, 1941, for Ukrainian Christmas, Sophie's parents, and siblings Alex and Millie came for a visit to celebrate Sviat Vechir (Christmas Eve). They brought Sophie a trunk and a tablecloth which they couldn't afford on her wedding day. They also gave them 2 cows and the $40 dollars in donations as wedding gifts. The $40 was used to buy a cream separator. Sophie and August were wise to invest in a cream separator because selling the cream brought in the extra cash needed to survive. Milking was done every day by hand and the cream shipped to Saskatoon, Saskatchewan about 80 kilometres by train to the dairy; the milk money was used to buy the necessary staples.

*Modern day Ukrainian Christmas Eve
setting Sviat Vechir at my sister Angie's house.*

So happy together

A few years before meeting Sophie, in 1938, August had purchased three quarters of a section of farmland from George Kertan. Later, he purchased one more quarter of land, and he and Sophie raised 10 children on the farm. As a new bride, Sophie came with many expectations such as having a family, growing a huge garden and paying off their farm as they started a new life together. The farm was paid off in eleven years with no interest paid as it was a private sale and they did not purchase it from a bank but paid it off in time with their written agreement.

*Our old farm where I grew up
located 12.9 kilometres east of Hanley and 12.9 kilometres north of Kenaston Saskatchewan. It was sold in 1973 and all the buildings removed.*

*Headstone of my parent's
August and Sophie (Dubyk)Mutala.
Buried at Kenaston, Saskatchewan.*

Until death parted them

Sophie (Dubyk) Mutala was an example of the spirited Ukrainian pioneer women who believed "hard work never hurt you." She found her Prince in August and though they had many hard times, they were always together. Both loved to dance, play cards, play the harmonica, sing and socialize. They were married for 42 years when August died at the age of 77 years from a heart attack. Sophie cried and cried: she had lost the love of her life and never did remarry. Whenever she rocked her grandson to sleep, Sophie would sing, Bye, Bye, Love, a song by the Everly Brothers.

Creamy, White Gold

I still remember the process. It is ingrained in my memory, like my name. My mother would walk down our little valley from our old wooden yellow house to the big red barn, carrying two silver metal pails; then she'd get her three-legged stool and balance on it like a person practising the treetop pose in yoga. She would then proceed to milk both Bossy and Brownie.

The cows sometimes co-operated and sometimes did not, being moody like a woman during her menstrual cycle. Our farm was 12.9 kilometres east of Hanley and 12.9 kilometres north of Kenaston, Saskatchewan. The separator room was an old room connected to the porch of our house. My parents were married on November 2, 1940. They received two cows and 40 dollars as gifts for their wedding and invested this money in a cream separator. Minimum wage was 30 cents an hour then, milk cost 52 cents a gallon and coffee was five cents a cup.

The separator, with its two separate spouts, was big and it sat on the floor. When you poured the milk into the large silver bowl and turned the wooden handle, out came the milk from one spout and the rich, pure cream from the other. Mmm, is there anything as tasty as the one hundred per cent pure, rich farm cream with no additives or preservatives?

I was the observer, and I watched my mother start to squeeze the cow's teats… squish, squish, the milk hitting the metal pail. The first few drops create a remarkable unique sound, almost indescribable – a tin-like tinkle. I can still hear that sound today.

Swish, swish went the cow's tail and soon our black cat, Toby, came for her share of the feast. My mother, Sophie, so in tune with her strokes, without looking up or a rhythm change, squirted our cat in the face and then continued milking, her job just beginning.

Our cat, loving and hating every minute of the milk dripping from her face into her mouth, was happy for the warm, frothy milk but maybe would have preferred it in a dish. Her milk bath running down her face, she loved the opportunity to self-clean.

The pails full, mom would give the old cows a gentle tap on their backs and we would walk back to the house carrying two pails of that frothy looking white gold.

Yes, gold it was, as the pioneers lived off the income from the cream that came from that milk. "Pin money" it was called in the old days, as women pinned the money to their bras and kept it for rainy days. It was often the only cash that a woman had to her name. The men in those days controlled the bank accounts. Yet my mom and dad, Sophie and August Mutala, used cream money to buy staples like sugar, fresh fruit for canning and preserves, and many extra items that the farm did not produce but were needed to raise their 10 children.

The cream was then placed into two metal cans, labelled with a number and our family name, and sent from our farm to Saskatoon, Saskatchewan by train 80 kilometres away. A man picked up the cream cans we placed on the road by our farmhouse that were to be shipped from the farm each morning. In winter, the cream was stored in an old shed that had been converted to an ice shed. Ice was cut from the slough with an old pick, and the ice was placed in the cement-floor shed.

Sometimes wood chips or straw were added to insulate the ice. In summer, the cream container was placed in a dirt hole; the ice melted into ice-cold water, keeping the cream cold.

We also made butter from day-old cream by placing it in a glass quart-sealer jar and shaking it until the cream churned into butter. A little salt was added for flavour at the end of the process.

My mom was an excellent cook. She used to make homemade bread that melted in your mouth served with fresh butter, cream cake or chocolate cake with caramel icing made from brown sugar and cream.

Nothing went to waste. Cottage cheese, using the skim milk, was often cooked slowly on the back of the woodstove in a pot. Yes, good income, very hard work everyday, but well worth the effort as we were never hungry growing up.

Cows grazing in a field.

Liquid gold, cream was how the pioneers survived their many years on the farm sometime receiving twenty-five dollars for a big can of cream. Twenty-five dollars was a lot of money in those days. Bread was 8 cents a loaf so you could buy 32 loaves of bread with that money or about 30 lbs of sugar as 10 lbs were sold for 7.34 a lb. My six sisters, three brothers and I were the grateful recipients of the results of that creamy, white gold.

Mud Pies

Mud pies, mud pies, hear my cry
I love mud pies
That's no lie
Squish'em, Mix' em
Hold them high
Mud pies, mud pies
Do or Die
My favourite reply

Crash– the lighting streaked across the sky. A hiss, a snap, and then a bang. A sizzle then a boom! That was a close one. Another horrific, electrical storm hits sunny Saskatchewan. After a weeklong of plus 30 degrees Celsius, it was bound to happen. I peeked out to watch now and then from my usual hiding place– in bed under the covers. One gets so hot under the covers that your hair gets wet and the sweat starts dripping down your cheeks. You are forced to come up occasionally for a bit of air.

Storms in Saskatchewan could be fierce and with the heat built up it became hot, and dry. Ravaging well into the night, making sleep near impossible, and each crack of lightning brought a gigantic crossfire boom. I jumped and wanted to crawl out of my skin.

My sister, Angie was snoring beside me and I snuggled a little closer to her for protection from the storm. Finally, my eyes became so heavy with sleep that I drifted off to the echo of lightning bolts in my ears.

"Wow! Look at all this good stuff over here," I hear shouting. "This is better over here," more shouting. My eyes were so heavy, and I felt exhausted from a fitful sleep. What was all the screaming and yelling out the window. As I pried open my eyes I tried to figure out where I was and what was happening.

I quickly got up realizing we had company, stumbling sleepily down the stair's half dressing on the way as I wouldn't want to miss out on the action. Diane and Darlene, my cousins shouted together at me that it rained last night and look at all this glorious mud. "It's about time you got up."

"Marion, you sleepyhead you'll miss out on the cooking. Hurry up dig in; we are having a blast."

They talked so fast and on cue together one could not tell the difference between the twins. Short, sassy blonde hair, blue eyes, and grinning from ear to ear with their hands and bare feet wrapped in a mud bath. They were having fun.

I felt bad as I had overslept and was missing out on all the fun. "Let's do this," they shouted simultaneously "the mud is perfect now. It is the, softest gooiest, and squishiest and most fun now before the hot sun dries it."

"Wasn't that an awesome storm last night, fierce and beautiful? I love those loud cracks and booms." Angie said.

Unlike me, my cousins and sister were not afraid of electrical storms. "This is a baker's paradise," squealed Angie. "Go get some eggs Marion, quick. It's gonna be another scorcher and we want to get all this baking done before the mud becomes too hard."

I ran to the chicken coop feeling like I never slept a wink and recalled the storm from last night. A shiver ran up my spine. I grabbed an old, tin bowl and proceeded to fill it with eggs knowing full well I could take about six eggs without mom saying anything but any more than that and I could get into big trouble. I carefully placed the eggs into the bowl slowly, and then hurriedly prodded up the hill. The girls were getting the best mud off my aunt and uncle's car right near the mud flaps. When you drive your car over dirt roads after a rain, the excellent mud stores around the flaps near the tires.

"Awesome," I said to my cousins, "peel that chunk right there. Perfect!"

We proceeded to build the most perfect mud pies crying, "Mud pies, mud pies hear my cry! I love mud pies it's no lie. Squish 'em, mash 'em, hold them high, mud pies, mud pies. Do or die, my favourite reply."

Many children, especially farm children, from different cultures make mud pies. This is not unique to Ukrainian traditions. Want to know the secret to the best mud pies in Saskatchewan?

The secret to a good mud pie is grab some glorious mud from the wheel frame of a car after a hard rain. Add 1 egg and mix 'em till the texture feels soft, and gooey. Shape into round, small pies and let dry in the sun. Voila, mud pies to die for. But don't tell my sister or my twin cousins I disclosed the secret recipe. They will splatter me with mud from head to toe.

*Stained Glass Pioneer Picture by Rodney Ketsa
taken at Vegreville, Alberta Monument.
See page v for more info.*

Turkey Torment

There I was… waiting, just waiting by the screen door. If I waited long enough, perhaps, just perhaps, they would waddle down the hill towards the barn. Should I go now or wait?

The sweat was wringing off my forehead and my stomach was queasy.

Ok now, go, run. Like a deer, I shot off heading full speed. No, this was not a race, but perhaps the start of my training for an athletic career as I did end up being good at track and field

Birds in a Saskatchewan Slough on a Farm.

in school and was captain of my basketball and volleyball teams. I did win a crest and many red ribbons for the 45.72 metre dash.

Farm life is not just clean air and fresh water. We had an outhouse. My mad dash was to use the outhouse. And we had turkeys and chickens that ran freely in the yard. Free range poultry like today, in the store, it costs you extra. Well, those free range were at my expense and as a small child those poultry were larger than me. Those turkeys would gobble around and peck you to death given the opportunity. It was downright horrifying. Perhaps, I have turkeys to thanks for my athleticism.

I was running as fast as I could on the path of least resistance and suddenly, I was down on the ground. I had tripped and fallen over a wooden rocking horse, my dad August made for us as a child.

Before, I could get up, I was attacked by a bunch of critters climbing and pecking on top of me from all directions. Luckily, my mom heard my screams and shooed them off, otherwise I might not be here to tell my tormented tale of turkeys.

Gobble, gobble! Revenge can be sweet and every time I eat a delicious turkey dinner I do so with a big smile.

50 Loads of Hay

Our old red barn was more than a home for the mice, cats and cows. What was so cool about this old barn is that it had a lovely hayloft. It was our playhouse. I still can picture myself there with my baby brother Eddie, romping in the hayloft. What an incredible time! No toys for us as we made our own enjoyment. Fun in the hayloft.

Every fall, during haying season dad would take the old tractor and swath the hay into neat rows and then pick it up and put it on his hay wagon. I'm sure he would do at least 50 loads of hay in order to have enough feed for his milking cows and pigs. Dad used to cut the hay to feed cattle and stored it in the top part of the barn. There was a hole in the top ceiling of the barn and when he wanted to feed the cows, he just pushed it with a fork down the hole to feed his cattle. He would even make some into square bales and use binder twine to secure. I can visualize the square bales neatly stacked.

We knew better... do not disturb those bales. The loose hay pile was used to feed the cattle below and that hole in the ceiling became our spy hole. Watching, observing family members below at work, tossing down feed to the cows below. Old Bossy or Bessy or Blackie. These memories are engrained in my soul. The smell of hay puts me there.

We had this great old red barn built in 1954, the same year as my sister was born. This is often how big families kept track of time with the birth of siblings. The new house in Hanley was built the year I was born 1957. When we sold the farm, the new owner sold the old red barn to a farmer near Hanley on an acreage. It still stands there and looks so small and forlorn.

My younger brother and I thought that barn was paradise. We would jump, run and fall into that hay loft. I still remember the dust, musty but fascinating smell of nature. The other great feature of that barn was the door at the top of the barn slid open sideways and then we could jump from the top of the hayloft to the ground either landing on bales or piles of hay.

*Our old red barn built in 1954
was sold and moved from the farm
when our farm was sold to an acreage
1.6 kilometres south near Hanley, Saskatchewan.*

Round Bale taken near David Dubyk, my cousin's farm near Kenaston, Saskatchewan, 0.80 kilometres east of our farm.

There was nothing like having a good workout falling from the top of hayloft to the ground. Perhaps, that is why I am not scared of heights today. The height of our barn was 2-3 metres tall. Sometimes we would ride the calves. We would jump on the calves from the top loft of the barn. Or if we rode the pigs, we would jump on them from the top of their wooden slated shelter. Unsafe? Maybe, but still loads of fun.

How many bales can you make with 1 wagon of hay? I am

guessing about 100 bales as a full truck and trailer load of hay is about 512 bales and a half load is about 256 bales or 12-13 tons of hay.

$6.00 a square bale seems to be the price for one square bale today. A good square bale was more like $2.00 when my dad was farming during the 70's, one wonders how many bales can be made from 50 loads of hay?

50 loads might be about 500 bales, but it is extremely easy to make the bales now compared to when my dad was farming. It was all done by hand then and baling today, is done by machine. My dad would have had to work all week to do the haying and baling to get enough feed to store and feed the animals for winter. Then there was the physical labour of doing chores everyday.

Farmers work hard to feed us and at $2.00 a bale or even $6.00 a bale this never equates to the labour-intensive activity or hourly rate a person makes at another job. So, thank a farmer.

The work on the land, harvesting hay still brings an unforgettable feeling every autumn. There is nothing like sleeping on a fresh pile of hay.

My Place, My Pillow

"There are strange things done in the midnight sun" so starts Robert W. Service in his poem, "The Cremation of Sam McGee." None were stranger to me than the strange family rule of "my place, my pillow."

Growing up on the Mutala family farm in rural Saskatchewan, I thought it was a commonplace rule. I asked my friends about this strange rule. They grew up in even bigger families than me with 12 or 16 children; ours was slightly smaller with only 10 children but they had not heard of this rule.

Then I asked my cousins with smaller families. They too, had not heard of this rule. I started to think that perhaps it was a district or a county rule, but no one had heard of it. As a matter of fact, everyone that I asked outside of our family had never heard of the rule. "My place, my pillow."

I tried to find out from my nine brothers and sisters how the rule became established. No one seemed to know or maybe they were just not telling. There were a few theories thrown around.

Maybe Ernie, the oldest boy, wanted to watch baseball on our old black-and-white TV and might have established the rule. Or the lack of seating spaces in our living room might have been the reason. I asked Ernie who might have enforced the rule. He had no clue where it came from. My three older sisters said the rule never existed when they were living at home.

There was an 18-year age span from the oldest to the youngest child in our family. All the players – including my

Blue Hills School Sign as school torn down. 1.6 kilometres east from our farm. My older sisters Margaret, Evelyn, Angie and Pat and brother Ernie went to school there.

sisters and brothers that still lived at home; like me, just had to play along. That rule was embedded in our family history and tradition by the time we were born.

When I discussed the rule with my own three children, they said that it sounded like the "Shotgun" rule to get the best spot on the passenger side in the front seat of a vehicle. I argued with them that although calling "Shotgun" might be a similar idea and was a rule that also worked; it still was not quite like the "My place, my pillow" iron-clad phrase that existed on our family farm – a rule that for some reason everyone knew, obeyed and respected.

The crazy thing about this rule that still amazes me today, as an adult, is that there were never any questions asked, no discussion, and no arguments about the rule. It was as if it was a holy grail never to be disobeyed.

"My place, my pillow."

It was magic. When you had to get up to go get a drink, go to the bathroom, or for whatever reason... as long as you said, "My place, my pillow" before you left your seat, it was respected and your favourite chair or the best seat was yours when you came back.

However, if you forgot to say, "My place, my pillow" before you got up... well, as they say, all's fair in love and war. That chair was fair game and up for grabs and would not be yours when you returned. There was no time limit, even if you left for a long time.

"My place, my pillow," says Marion, as she gets up and leisurely strolls away from her comfy La-Z-Boy that everyone envied.

The Great Pyrohy Eat Off

There are many food contests in the world. They seem to be challenges of enormous magnitude. To name just a few there is the Hot Chili Pepper Eating contest in Vancouver, British Columbia. There is the Garlic Eating Challenge or Nathan's Famous Hotdogs in New York City, U.S.A. There is the World Pie Eating Contest in Wigan in Northwest England and then there is our very own Saskatoon, Saskatchewan's King of Kovbasa eating contest.

These local and national eating contests are pale in comparison to the great pyrohy eating contest my baby brother challenged my brother-in-law to in the spring of 1973. Yes, he was my baby brother, but a baby he was not. Eddie was the youngest child in our family of 10 and the youngest boy of three, but as fate would have it, he turned out to be the giant of the siblings.

His full height reached 1.93 metres tall and he weighed about 90 kilograms. By today's standards not really that big, I have two nephews taller at 1.98 metres. Remember, this was years before the extra-large shoes in stores and the National Basketball Association with their mega-sized basketball players from the States. This was small-town-Saskatchewan, in the sixties and large-size shoes were unavailable to us country folk.

I was not at the actual contest, but the "word on the street" was he challenged my brother-in-law, to a perogy meltdown, an eatery, to decide who could eat a maximum number of those white, delicate morsels for supper. This too, was before the introduction of mega meals, the super gulps and the great buffet of China smorgasbords introduced to our North American diet.

Pyrohy-varenyky-perogies are considered the number one favourite food in Canada. I read in the Saskatoon Star Phoenix, a survey which stated perogies were the number one favourite food in Western Canada as many cultures besides Ukrainians eat a dumpling of some sort.

Bowl of pyrohy or varenyky, or perogies.

My perspective of the contest could be skewed as I was not present to the entire affair. I am telling the story through the eyes of my mother, Sophie and two sisters who witnessed the whole gall darn episode.

Since my dad's and my mother's passing as well as my one sister, three of the primary witnesses are gone, so I am replaying this contest entirely from what they shared with me. That fateful day took place in Vancouver, British Columbia when my mom and dad were visiting my older sister. It was Easter and springtime and we had survived another long cold winter in Saskatchewan.

My mother of Ukrainian descent would often take it upon herself to make perogies. This was a normal operation for her. If Sophie came to visit, she would take over your kitchen and start cooking because that was her nature. For mom, to go on a holiday to someone's house and spend the day making pyrohy as she called them was not strange. We ate perogies, at least once a week while we were growing up. She would say, "Yisty, Yisty, eat, eat," one moment and the next second, "Do not eat too much or you will get fat."

When Sophie started to make varenyky it was a task and a full day's work. She would put on her babushka, tie it to the back of her head and accompany it with her baba or grandmother apron. A baba brooch of flour was often located

My mother Sophie (Dubyk) Mutala with her babushka.

on her apron dead centre. She would proceed to clear off the entire kitchen table in order to get down to work.

This was no easy task and perogy-making was serious business. Sophie was a careful cook having survived "The Great Depression" and had known hunger pains in her life growing up near Hafford, Saskatchewan with four brothers and two sisters. Her kitchen was her domain and on rare occasions she let us cook.

Let us proceed with the perogy contest...

On one side, you have my 15-year-old, hormonal brother, going through pukerty, growing, growing, growing and hungry, hungry, hungry, all the time. I remember when he came home from basketball practice, he would go straight to the fridge and drink an entire milk jug straight from the gallon, kind of like a shooter, a shot of horilka or Ukrainian homebrew. Straight up and down it went in its entirety. He would then munch on a whole brick of solid, yellow, cheddar cheese for a snack.

In the other corner, we have my big, brother-in law, a full adult male about 40 years old, 1.93 metres, 92 kilograms and size 12 shoes. To protect the innocent, let us call him Mykolai or Mikey as you know he eats anything. A fully grown garbage gut.

One might think the challenge was one-sided, a 15-year-old versus a 40-year-old. However, knowing both contestants, the challenge was fair, and the opponents were on equal footing. It was not as if one had the advantage over the other... a lightweight, fighting a heavyweight... the size unequal but the appetite for food was fully charged. Let us call my brother, Rocky now for short as he changed his name in later years to Rock Edward.

So, let the eat-off begin. Tak, yes, Sophie was in fine form and could keep up with the best of them, working furiously in the kitchen cutting the dough into small balls, rolling each ball round, then flattening each ball separately with her wooden rolling pin, filling those perfect sized perogies with either cottage cheese and potatoes, sauerkraut and even plums.

Take a purple plum cut it in half, take out the seed and then put one half in the perogy dough. Plum pyrohy! Duzhe dobra. Eat with sour cream. Rocky and Mykolai are wolfing them down... consuming them by the dozens.

A normal perogy dough recipe consists of:
2 1/2 cups flour, 1 egg well beaten, 1/2 tsp. salt and 2 tbsp oil and enough warm water to make a soft dough

For mom, her recipes start with a large bowl of flour. Then she proceeds from there.

(*Warning about six cups of flour makes roughly 400 perogies*)

Let the countdown begin...Odyn, one, dva, two, treh, three... next a finger count, finally resort to paper, four sticks and a line crossed through for every five perogies. No mistakes in counting could be made. I am sure August; my dad was doing the counting for he was always up for a good challenge.

The two contestants were not eating any meat, or cabbage rolls, sticking with just perogies. It was a pyrohy eating contest. So, they ate and ate... thirty each and still counting.

I love my perogies and in my youth and maybe even today, I could eat a dozen of mom's delicious duzhe dobre, very good perogies. If I was hungry, I could eat maybe two dozen as I like my food and love perogies. However, the more one eats of those critters, the more stuffed one gets and soon the stomach is starting to feel like lead and sleepiness takes over. 30 would be my limit.

Imagine, Sophie's dilemma. She loves it when people eat her food as it is a compliment to her culinary ability. But to keep up with these hungry guys…after 50 each I think even Sophie would roll her eyes and say that is enough. Not because she wants you to be hungry but at 75 perogies each I could see her shaking her head and say, "Chiki, Chiki, just you wait and see."

Hitting 90 a piece, mom would certainly shout "Yoi" and know she was feeding a couple of oinkers and at 95 for sure she would say something to the effect like save some for the starving people in the world.

Make no mistake, a family challenge, is a family challenge and determination sets in at the end. Once Rocky set his mind to the task, his goal of 100 perogies would be reached and Rock Edward was determined to meet the finish line. The sweet sound of 100 to Rocky's ears was apparent as he imagined the cheers at the finish line. Mykolai coming in a close second, only able to eat 99, tossed in his fork.

What happened next, I cannot say, having not been there that fate-filled day. But as sure as my name is Marusia, I will always remember and hear about that perogy contest of 1973. Family functions are the time to brag and do silly things. As sure as Ukrainian-Canadians starting immigrating to Canada in 1891, the winner that day was a 15-year-old boy from Kenaston, Saskatchewan, a provincial basketball player and fantastic guitar picker, my brother Eddie, Rock Edward, stage name Bigfoot.

I speak the truth. No word of a lie.

Connected

Even though I grew up on a farm near Hanley/Kenaston, Saskatchewan, I have been a city slicker for quite a while. I still feel a strange and loving connection to the flat open land of my childhood. Psychologists say that the first few years of your life are critical and formative for your personality. My memories on the farm remain vivid and true.

There is nothing like driving out in the country. Often, I travel to view farmlands, crops and the countryside. Saskatchewan is known for the flat prairie jokes like, you can watch your dog run away for miles and farmers are outstanding in their fields. To me, seeing flat prairie land is a good thing.

Thank a farmer for the lovely wheat grown in Saskatchewan fields.

It's so refreshing, and such a feeling of peace and joy warms my heart to see trees, flowers, sloughs, vegetation and cattails. I often wonder what the story was behind the people who lived in an old run-down farmyard or house as I pass by. I wish I could have been a fly on the wall to have heard their old tales and understand their history and hardships. Not to judge, but I'm in awe at how the pioneers survived the isolation, cold, dark winters with stark heating, no electricity, no neighbours close by, and no cars to run to town on a whim's notice. They would often work 10-hour days just for basic survival needs of food, shelter and clothing.

I wonder if I could have survived as I love my warm showers and heat and underground parking. My home overlooks 220 acres of walking trails. I have my own golden pond that I view daily from my windows where the ducks play and even on occasion the pelicans visit. So, I feel at home.

Baby Ducks by a Pond in Saskatoon, Saskatchewan

My Aunt Anne and Uncle Nick Dubyk (my mom's brother's) old farmhouse, 0.80 kilometres, south from our old farmhouse.

Nature settles the beast within and even though I didn't marry a farmer as my mother, Sophie, did and wanted me to, the farm will always be in my blood. You can take the girl out of the country, but you cannot take the country out of the girl. I will always feel connected to this big sky prairie land. The flat prairie connection shares a permanent place in my soul.

Chasing the Divine

I grew up dirt poor, not starving by any means, but wore hand me downs from six older sisters and lived in an old house with no running water or indoor plumbing. Yet, I feel rich and believe by today's standards; that I received an inheritance that sustains me through any dark nights.

Rich in faith. This faith was passed on from both my parents and grandparents, so no chasing of the divine was necessary. It was an inherited gift, and I am grateful. This faith has made me aware that God provides "what we need" not "what we want." I feel no envy about material possessions, or my neighbours and this gift gives me the ability to live a blessed, simple life.

Faith is the greatest gift of inheritance any parent can pass on to their child and I am so glad I received that internal blessing. I did not know my grandparents as my dad emigrated from Slovakia in 1930. My mother's parents emigrated from Ukraine, however, my dido or grandfather died before I was born, and my baba or grandmother died when I was four.

Because of my parent's actions, my mother and father took me to church Sundays and lived a good faith-filled life; this tells me a lot about their upbringing as well. On the farm, growing up, we often said the rosary together as a family on our knees in the dark, before going to bed.

I never got the Barbie doll I wanted as a child. I never got fancy clothes or went on elaborate holidays. However, I did get a precious gift of divine life and faith.

How does my active faith, continue to define or refine my life? Well, I hear the meadowlark singing, the flowers blooming, and the sun fills my life. I am truly grateful to be alive and enjoy each day. A belief in an active God causes me great satisfaction in my soul. I live relatively worry free and am not sold on material goods. My relationships with others are strong and deep and self-awareness allows me to "let go and let God."

Rainbow near Saskatoon, Saskatchewan.

I have a simple philosophy which I play out in my daily life and that is, be kind to others and to do "the little things with love" as Mother Teresa suggested. To be able to live simply or simply live is very freeing and on those terrifying "dark nights of the soul" those nights that never seem to end, I pray. My life is one big prayer to God and God is often in my thoughts.

So, by contemporary Canadian standards, my faith allows me to fully live and enjoy every day, not worry about tomorrow and receive each blessing. I am extremely grateful for my inherited gift of faith. One sometimes thinks faith is not passed on or needs to be chased.

I usually bless my children before they leave my place with the sign of the cross and ask God to protect them. My three adult children, at this point in their lives are not regular church goers but are very spiritual and good people. On one of those rare occasions when they were leaving, I forgot to bless them and they said, "Mom, you forgot to bless me."

I knew at that moment, perhaps, just perhaps, they too have inherited my gift of faith and have no need to chase the divine.

Compote of stewed fruit called Uzvar considered God's drink served last during Ukrainian Christmas Eve supper Sviat Vechir.

What History Teaches Us About Soil?

My brother Don, use to put worms, salamanders or frogs down my back. Not a pleasant thought at anytime, but to a child of three or four, it was traumatic. Perhaps, that is why I failed my Biology 102 lab as I refused to touch, let alone cut open, a live formaldehyde frog to watch its heartbeat. Ask me why I am still scared of worms, salamanders and frogs to this day?

During the Second World War, the Germans were hauling truckloads of soil from Ukraine to Germany. Why would they do that? Ukraine has some of the blackest, fertile soil in the world and has been considered "the breadbasket of Europe." Why else would Ukraine have been invaded and conquered so many times?

What does history teach us about soil? How can we use this information in Canada and more specifically Saskatchewan? Saskatchewan has been noted for being the largest agricultural producer and exporter in the world with potential to "feed the world."

When my father, August was farming during the period of 1930 to 1970's he encountered all kinds of problems, especially with his soil blowing away. He would cultivate the soil and let it sit idle for a year rotating crops. But the wind would blow the dirt from our fields and coat our windowsill ledges on the farm, much to the chagrin of my mother Sophie, who had to dust all the time. We have learned our lesson about cultivation and studied better ways to farm since then.

What are the ways in the 21st century that we can enrich and protect our soil naturally to produce maximum usage? How can we increase yields and produce with that beloved black, rich moisture soil?

I figure water irrigation and earthworms. Call me crazy, but what do Slavic and Ukrainians know about earthworms and water? Well, my dad, August appreciated all nature and my mom, Sophie loved it when she saw earthworms in her garden commenting on how rich they made her soil. And my uncles loved using earthworms for fishing.

Worms increase the amount of air and water that gets into the soil. By breaking up organic matter, through eating, earthworms can leave a very valuable type of fertilizer to enrich the soil. What better farm labourers than harvesting earthworms – way cheaper than using chemicals and purchasing fertilizers.

I would bet my last penny; you could get a Canadian Agriculture grant to study and open an operating earthworm farm through the University of Saskatchewan Research Department. Laugh all you want, but I wonder what is the cost of an earthworm and is there a market for earthworm farms?

"At the moment, red worms on Amazon.com sell for about $9 for 300. Night crawlers from family operations sell for about $30 to $32 per pound. You'll sell about 350 to 400-night crawlers per pound, so you'll be getting approximately $0.08 each if you sell them retail in bulk." *www.thepennyhoarder.com*

Earthworms are natural cultivators and move through the soil. They are like miniature little plows tunneling their way underground allowing air and water to get to the roots of plants. Crops are in desperate need of air and water. Dry and compacted soil does not produce great crops. The diet the earthworms eats, and discharges is an available and balanced form of nutrition for your crops and soil.

What do we know about the earthworms? The Common

Earthworm or its Scientific Name: Lubricous terrestrosin is an herbivore and can live up to six years and grows up to 0.356 metres long. That is one huge underground burrowing worm. Of the 180 earthworm species found in the United States and Canada, only 60 are invasive and their skin is very lubricant, so more investigation is needed.

It would be interesting to study and invest in further development of earthworm farms to explore the benefits of a high earthworm population in the soil. It could be a curious undertaking and worth taking a good look at what Mother Nature produces naturally.

If you are not ready for an earthworm farm; just by reducing tillage, planting cover crops, utilizing crop residues you can increase the earthworm population naturally. In addition, you should make every effort to reduce compaction in the field, by perhaps using a combination of a water irrigation system and introducing earthworms as natural fertilizers that will enhance your soil life.

Prairie Thistle

However, do not be hasty and start cutting earthworms in half to increase their yield as apparently the popular believe of cutting them in half will not produce two earthworms. That is just a myth.

And if starting an earthworm farm makes you feel a little crawly, you can always go out to your "garden to eat worms" as some people might find them a refreshing treat. You also will attract many great fisherman friends who will always "love you" for having their necessary source of bait.

This is just one wormy way to improve your soil and friendships and appears to me to be one natural win/win situation all around. It might even save you some cash and who does not want to save money as well as preserve and enrich our soil and the environment.

Outdoor stook or sheaf of wheat a didukh which means grandfather used for Ukrainian Christmas Eve or Sviat Vechir. Many early Ukrainian immigrants were farmers as were my granparents and parents symbolic of agricultural background. Wheat and bread are huge part of Ukrainian culture.

The Five F's

The Gift of Faith

Wouldn't it be nice if Christmas were a spirit of kindness that exists all year long? One of the greatest gifts, I received from my parents, Sophie (Dubyk) and August Mutala was the gift of faith. In baba's trunk, my grandparents, Dido Stefan Dubyk, Baba Tessie Woznakowski and like many other emigrants, did not have room to bring many items from Ukraine in 1911/1912.

The remains of their empty trunks we used as our childhood play trunks. I'm not positive what was in my Baba's trunk on arrival to Canada. Growing up under my parent's roof, however, gives light to the fact, that my baba's trunk must have contained religious artifacts like an icon, a bible and a rosary.

My Baba or grandmother died when I was four years old, so I don't remember her, and my Dido or grandfather died before I was born so I can tell you very little about their faith. However, my mom and dad's faith spoke volumes as we went to church every Sunday rain or shine, prayed the rosary on our knees when we were small and were members regularly supporting our parish.

What will you pass on to your children? Perhaps you have a large bank account or copious amounts of material possessions. Besides culture, traditions and their heritage, many Ukrainians pass on spiritual faith.

Tak, yes, their faith, one of the five "F's." Faith, family, food, friends and fun; vital and key to a fulfilling life, faith being the first "F."

*3 loaves of kolach bread with a candle
is symbolic of the Holy Trinity and Christ our light,
used for Ukrainian Christmas Eve or Sviat Vechir.*

The Second "F"

A time for new beginnings, Lent gives us that opportunity to start fresh. For me, I continue to ponder ideas that are healthy for living like my Baba's Borsch... which gives food for body and food for the soul. I had suggested the five "F's" faith, family, food, friends and fun as being important to a fulfilling life.

So, let us discuss the second "F" which is family. Family, tak, yes, all those jokes about family, for example, you can pick your friends but not your relatives.

I was blessed to have grown up on a farm and had a lot of siblings, nine to be exact. Maybe, I did not always appreciate them growing up, but realize now; coming from a large family, it is a mixed blessing. I have six sisters (one deceased) and three brothers.

Depending on each person's perception, if you asked each of my siblings, "What was it like growing up in a large Catholic family?" the answer would differ significantly. As the youngest girl and second youngest in the family it had its pluses and minuses.

From my older sister's perspective, they would say I was spoiled. However, from my eyes, they had the advantage of being older, with more privileges and liked to boss me around. If I did not act a certain way, they would not let me hang out. You mature fast in a family of 10 and truth be known, "Really, can anyone be spoiled in a family that size?"

My Two Sisters and Myself in Our Ukrainian Blouses.
From left to right Marion Mutala, Margaret Bells, Angie Wollbaum

Growing up on a farm, we all had to pick rocks and pick peas. But then again; we got to watch those wonderful afternoon matinees together, while shelling those huge tubs of peas.

Some things our family did learn very quickly was to get along, share and solve our own problems. Mom and dad were much too busy keeping us fed and clothed to get involved in our disputes. A big family teaches you a lot of life lessons and how-to problem solve. There was a shortage of personal space in our house, so we were often outdoors and really had to learn to survive together.

Pray, work, eat, play, rest together. Saying the rosary in the evening, together on our knees, teaches you a lot. And then the next day, we would start over again.

Feed your soul and have faith with your family with Baba's Borsch... food for thought.

My three sisters, my brother and me.
Our singing group called The Sassy Sisters and my brother Ernie.
From left to right Marion Mutala on guitar, Alene Mutala on washboard,
Ernie Mutala on guitar, Angie Wollbaum on accordion and Margaret Bells on banjo.

My Dad, August Mutala with his two grandchildren Symret and Brian.

Dubyk Reunion in Front of Our Grandparents Stefan Dubyk and Tessie (Woznakowski) Dubyk's old farmhouse by Hafford, Saskatchewan.

Baba's Borsch

Mmm… I can still smell the dill, the vinegar, and the fresh scent of borsch on my tongue, filling my nose, my senses alive, and the thought invigorating. It is that time of year again and the produce from the garden is ready, the red beets ripe to make Ukrainian beet borsch.

I can still picture my mother, getting up early with her boxed dress on and slacks underneath going to her garden, her store, to pick all her homegrown vegetables, back-breaking work and then carrying them in her baba's apron and washtub to our farmhouse.

The preparation begins. Washing the vegetables in her kitchen sink, Sophie pulls out her blue metal canner soup pot with the white flakes on it and starts the endless task of cutting, slicing, dicing her vegetables and more importantly, the red beets which gives the Ukrainian borsch that unique red colour and flavour.

Caramelizing the onions in real butter Sophie adds boiling water, salt, pepper, and the vegetables one by one, 1 cup chopped potatoes, 1 cup shredded cabbage, 1/2 cup cut beans, 1/2 cup shelled peas, 1/2 cup sliced carrots, 4 medium-sized diced beets and the sprigs of dill, the biting dill flavour, the delicious aroma wafts and unfolds in her kitchen.

I can still taste my first spoonful.

Simmering the soup till the vegetables are just done, tender but firm, when it is finally ready, mama adds enough vinegar to taste at the end before adding the frothy real cream and serving it with her homemade bread and butter.

Picture my mama, babushka tied back behind her head, her stirring and tasting, a pinch of salt, a shake of pepper, the distinct flavour, the necessary dill and vinegar, getting it oh so right, oh so delicious and yes it contains and fills my Ukrainian soul.

Mmm... if only I had watched more closely, paid more attention.

Perhaps my borsch would taste better.

If only I had asked mom more questions.

If only Sophie was here to make me borsch, one last time,

If is such a sad word!

Borsch Soup with Dumplings

Braided Kolach Bread

Friends and Fun

Our family talked a lot. Everyone at the same time, so I am not sure if we exactly listened to each other. We also worked fast, ate fast, and did things quickly. Perhaps, so we could have more time to play, sing and have fun together with our friends. We were lucky all of us could sing, including our parents and eight out of 10 of us learned to play an instrument. Our parents could even play the harmonica. Music was a huge part of our lives.

That really is remarkable considering there were no private lessons in those days where we lived. Mom and dad bought an accordion and banjo for the older girls and then a guitar for the younger ones, so we taught ourselves. That was enough to get us started and create our own fun. We were not professional and could not read music, but we sure enjoyed singing and playing.

Marion Mutala and my sister,
Angie Wollbaum on accordion and my cousin Shirley Joubert
at one of my Book Launches.

Students from a Saskatoon High School with Marion Mutala playing her guitar at her Book Launch.

Often, we would sing till our fingers hurt from playing the guitar and we were so hoarse we could not talk.

Although, we are all busy now with our own families, my siblings and I still try and get together as often as we can to party and sing our hearts out in celebration.

What I have noticed about "All Things Ukrainian" besides culture, traditions, heritage, or spiritual faith many Ukrainians pass on the gift of music. My aunts and uncles on the Dubyk side sang and played musical instruments and even had a band that played at many weddings and on other occasions.

We were blessed to have my mom's two brothers Alex and Nick and their wives and families live on either side of my parent's farm which was 12.9 km east of the Hanley and 12.9 km north of Kenaston. So, we often spent time at each other's places. That was our entertainment and fun. And on a farm many friends would pop in at anytime for cards, coffee and a short visit. Our home was always a welcoming place.

My parents taught me to have faith, family, food and friends but also how to create your own fun, inexpensively. And therefore, I have a very healthy perspective on life which really helped me during Covid-19.

Tak, family, a blessing or a curse? I believe these Five F's are vital and the key to a fulfilling life.

During difficult times, have faith, call up a member of your family or a friend, make Baba's Borsch and feel free to feed your soul with music. Have fun together, celebrate each day... more insight and definitely food for life.

My 4 Sisters and One Brother with a Family Friend.
Back Row: Joan Anderson, Marion Mutala, Ernie Mutala, Alene Mutala
Front Row: Joyce Hayes, Marg Bells, Angie Wollbaum

The Blizzard

Last night, I was awakened by these weird, crackling noises and whistling sounds in the house. Something was happening outside. The wind was howling, and it felt cold in the house. I snuggled under my blankets and must have fallen back to sleep.

In the morning, I ran to the window to look outside and the ground was covered with freshly, fallen snow. Big mountains of snow. The wind was still blowing and making a screeching noise. The snow still proceeded to blow.

My mom said school was closed for today. "It's a blizzard out there."

I had rarely seen a blizzard like this one in the entire six years of my life. My sisters and brothers were still in bed and it was cold. I looked out the window again and could see that the air was frigid. It made me shiver. I was very glad to stay indoors. Mom made me some hot chocolate and lit the fire in our woodstove.

Mmm… that was very cozy. It was strange though to have both mom and dad in the house today, at the same time. They did not have to go out today as the buses weren't running to take students to school and the piles of snow made travel impossible. There were mountains of snow covering the buildings. Everything was shut down.

I looked out the window again and felt safe inside with my mom and dad. I was very thankful that I did not have to leave the house or go outside. The snow had been falling all night. It had arrived so suddenly and now covered everything and everywhere. It was cold, very cold, minus 30 degrees Celsius outside and the wind- chill brought the temperature down to minus 40 degrees Celsius. The wind was playing havoc, blowing this way and that way.

Dad and my mom decided to play a game of cards and have some more hot chocolate. My siblings and I did not even get dressed but lounged in our PJ's. It was great fun to be home with my family. We played all sorts of games like hide and seek; blocks, listened to music and the time just flew by.

Dad had to go feed the animals in the barn and attached a long twine rope from the barn to the house so he would not get lost coming back to the house.

My father explained that sometimes a person would get lost trying to find their way back to the house during a blizzard. During a complete white out, one might not even find the barn or the house again. A person could die in the cold if they got lost. So, it was an important safety precaution to use a rope and light candles in the house so one could see the light to find your way back. Our red barn was somewhat warm and gave enough protections for our animals, but a human might not survive the night there.

Soon it was suppertime, and the wind was still blowing but not as strong and it had finally stopped snowing. All in all, it had been a pretty good day for us inside. I wondered what would have happened to us if it snowed like that when we were at school.

Would we have to have slept overnight in the school? I was glad to be at home on a day like today. I was wondering when the next blizzard day might come. It was sure nice to be cozy at home with my parents and brothers and sisters safe and sound.

Wild Horses at Robinson Bay

Growing up in a big family did not give us the luxury of summer travels. Our yearly holiday experience was going to Watrous each summer to soak in the healing salt water at Manitou Beach by Watrous. This salt therapeutic water helped heal your mosquito bites if you soaked in it. Then we ended the day with a family wiener roast. Beautiful time and inexpensive.

However, I wanted my children to have a camping experience and stay in a tent overnight so we would travel to Robinson Bay by North Battleford. The lake there was clear, calm blue water not salty like Manitou. This last summer, though we had quite the experience.

"But mom, I saw them. Really three of them – big, beautiful horses, a white one, a black one and a brown one all standing drinking from the lake. They tilted their heads and saw me too. I saw them- really. They looked like wild horses running and free. I saw them stop to drink water from Jackfish Lake."

We were on holidays and just arrived at our campsite number 334 on the south side of the bay as it was so hilly, green and lush by the lake. This summertime attraction made it a great peaceful holiday get away. I was tired and hot from travelling all the way from Saskatoon, Saskatchewan since morning with two teenagers and a dog in a crowded station wagon packed for a week's tenting at Jackfish Lake north of North Battleford, about 139 kilometres away.

"Jacob I'm tired. Let's set up camp first and have something to eat. Then you can go and explore."

"But mom I saw them. I really saw them. We should go tell the camp officer. What if someone hurts them?"

My son the protectionist of all creatures. He loves animals and especially things that are helpless. I knew that at the precious age of 12 he would not leave me alone until we did something.

"Ok, we will drive to the main gate and report it to the camp director." We drove the five kilometres back slowly to the main entrance in the heat, no air conditioner and sweltering in the plus 30 degrees Celsius it was outside.

The lady at the front desk gave us a strange look when we drove up again and mentioned the horses to her.

"This has been a campsite and provincial park for 50 years. Are you sure you saw some horses?" she quizzed.

Jacob shouted adamantly from the backseat.

"Three of them black, white and brown and they were drinking water from the lake. Beautiful wild looking animals. I know they were wild because I saw them on TV in a movie – the same kind. Black Stallion it was called – the movie."

"Slow down, son," The desk officer said. "We can't understand you when you talk so fast."

My son was looking excited now standing up in the back seat and waving his arms around.

The lady at the desk proceeded to radio the camp officer.

"Wild horses" the radio blared back laughingly.

"I will go take a look for them." said the radioman.

Later that afternoon, at the beach we saw them. Horse

tracks, I mean, evidence that they had been there, coyote tracks as well probably tracking them and barefoot tracks — someone had been running barefoot on the sand. That was dangerous running down there barefoot as many sharp rocks and broken glass was left on the beach.

"I used to love going barefoot," I told Jacob. "The ground and sand between your toes. Now one has to be so careful. No respect."

"Hi there. This is Jacob. Did I mention my mom was kind of a health freak too? Anyway, she said that as they were my horses, if only that were true, I should take up the narrative. She said it was "A Twilight Zone" occurrence, whatever that is."

Mother was off on one of her tangents again about how people are wrecking the environment with all our garbage and pollution. She was right of course, but I wanted to find those horses and was in no mood to hear her lecture.

"Mom look at these tracks. See I told you, horse tracks and they are heading up the hill that way in the bushes. Mom can I go up there and look for them."

"Later, Jacob it is getting dark now. I did not bring a flashlight. Tomorrow we can get up early with your sister and start looking for them."

"Mom, you know Tasha won't go tracking in the bush. She doesn't like bugs. We should have brought my bro, Symret. He would go exploring with me, mom. Then you would not have to go along. You could work on your book, mom."

Mom was an aspiring author trying to break into the publisher's market with her first book.

"Jacob, for your safety I am coming too. You know I like hiking and exploring as much as you. Besides, maybe I can find some neat flowers or herbs to use."

The next morning dawned bright and early and true to her word my mom and I headed off on our journey to find those wild horses. After two hours of hiking, there they were. Three magnificent beasts drinking thirstily from the water at Robinson Bay. My cellphone captured their true beauty and graceful purity. Mom and I knew this was our little secret and we could tell the horses just wanted the freedom to be wild horses at Robinson Bay.

My mom's father was fond of horses and used them at first when he started farming for pulling tractors and equipment and then for travel with their buggies in wintertime. My grandfather August was trained as a saddler and could make or repair saddles or leather repairs for harnesses. Later on, when my mom moved off the farm, into the town of Kenaston he made and gave away sets of wooden horses and buggies as a remembrance of his farming days. I have a lovely set of them. He instilled in my mom and me a love of horses.

Do I Finally Have Your Attention?

(We were a very musical family and used to make up songs and skits and played school growing up. Perhaps that is why four of us girls became teachers. I loved to write and got my first guitar when I was 12 years-old and started writing songs and poems. In High School, we had an exceptional teacher, Mr. Mike Hertz who gave us creative writing assignments in his English class. That is when I imagined the possibility of being a writer.)

Walk with both feet forward
Yes, pick it up
It's your heart
Find a way
Keep going
Put out small fires
Put pieces together
Ignore petty gossip
It's your life
It's not fair
It's still not fair
Be kind
Do what you can
No perfect plan
Or life
Take charge
Let go

Enjoy
Gratitude
Love deeply
Faith
Family
Food
Friends
Fun
Purpose
Happiness
Love
Peace
Joy
Hope
The greatest is love
Yes, love – a complete gift
Live simple, simply live
Live well
Love deeply

*Beautiful Sunflower in Saskatoon, Saskatchewan.
Ukraine's National Flower*

Rant and Radical, Part of My Family Heritage

When I began teaching special education at St. Anne's School in Prince Albert, Saskatchewan in 1979 over 40 years ago, I did not have many classroom rules. I used to teach the Three R's: Respect yourself, Respect others and Respect the environment.

If a problem occurred in class, I asked my students if they had respected the Three "R's." Once they looked at the problem by looking at the Three Rs, – inevitably, the problem was solved. Today, I could add another "R" for Rant or Radical.

Perhaps a rant or two might save our planet; would that make me a radical?

David Suzuki's words, "If actually caring about Canada's natural environment makes me a "radical," sign me the hell up!", says Suzuki. (*Planet S January 26-February 8, 2012, Volume 10, Issue 11*)

If we become radicals in this environmental hell might it cause someone to hear or more importantly to listen? I wonder. What is it going to take to save this planet?

My mother, Sophie, recycled before recycling was even talked about and became a buzzword, being a survivor of the Great Depression does that for you. She washed every plastic bag, reused, saved every box, tin or plastic container and recycled them over and repeatedly, even washing our disposable plastic forks and spoons at large family gatherings. The plastic cottage cheese containers were Ukrainian Tupperware, or so we would joke, no fancy Tupperware for our family.

My father, August walked daily and picked up every piece of garbage around town, every bottle from beer or pop, broken or not, recycled, reused every bit of thread, wire, screw or nail; his workshop full of treasures he had found. He repaired our shoes, the fine shoemaker he was and when we grew out of them, we passed them on. Hand me downs were the norm in our family of 10 and the hole in our screen door was repaired with a white, thick thread dad reused.

No new clothes for me, number nine out of 10 children, the seventh daughter out of seven girls. My sisters still pass me their hand me downs. Reuse, recycle, repair, never wasting anything, that was the norm for the pioneers. Having little, they appreciated everything.

We enjoyed making paper doll cut-outs from the old Eaton's catalogue and my school Webster's Dictionary had a comment and contained signatures from all my older siblings, yes, all eight of them, missing only my younger brother's. I remember drooling and longing for new crayons, pencils and school supplies my peers had brought on the first day of school, mine were reused and recycled and broken.

Today, in this world of consumerism my own three, adult children laugh at me as I answer them on my last phone, a once slick, razor cell phone, the back lost on it (one cannot get another replacement for it as they are out of style) I thought it was so cool when I bought it. That lasted maybe a month before new technology, something cooler evolved.

"Why don't you just get a new phone? Throw it away my children say."

"This phone still works, I say, a phone rings and you answer it. It still works and does its job." (Not wanting to trash something before its time and fill our landfills, with extra waste with all this slightly old, new, technology) My kids roll their eyes at me, my laptop is ancient too.

Should we add another R and rant a little more or become radical like Suzuki?

Four R's – What will it take to keep our planet green and safe and make a better world?

I am keen for green. A green planet, I care about Canada's natural environment as well as the entire world's natural environment. Call me a radical, but if Suzuki is ignored, Canada's scientific guru, who will hear my rant or my parent's rant long after all those radicals are gone?

"Sign me the hell up!" make me a "radical" if it will really work.

Boona/Boon

My mom loved Nabob coffee perked on a wood-burning stove. To this day, I buy Nabob. This is not a coffee commercial; however, childhood memories and smells are powerful.

Mmm… the smell of fresh coffee invigorates my senses and percolates my soul. Nothing smells quite like a good cup of java in the morning. The taste of it really is nothing compared to the actual odour of the brewed beans. This fragrance makes me want to climb out of bed on those cold winter mornings in Saskatchewan just to have my morning fix.

Imagine, having the opportunity to participate in an African boona/boon or coffee ceremony with complete cultural aspects. The Ethiopians/Eritreans have such a ceremony and I have had the enormous pleasure of participating in this fine experience. North Americans often survive the day with fancy logo cups of coffee, the larger the cup the better. This keeps up productivity and gets people through difficult times.

The Ethiopians/Eritreans have a special coffee ceremony that is likely as old as coffee itself. In my family, coffee was served in the morning time only and especially for breakfast. Then we might have a coffee break later on but for supper and during the remainder of the evening we drank tea.

Unlike North American culture where we might drink coffee all day long; the Ethiopians/Eritreans reserve coffee for special times or company. Their ceremony includes roasting the freshly green beans on a small fire, praying over the beans, grinding, then brewing in a clay pot to boiling point. Three demi-tasse cups of coffee or strong expresso served over a period of two to three hours. Along with coffee, stories and laughs are shared served with fresh hambasha, their native bread and freshly roasted popcorn with salt, no butter, but perhaps dates or nuts on top.

The Ethiopian/Eritrean coffee ceremony has religious significance as three brews of small cups are significant perhaps related to the Trinity in their Orthodox Christian faith, the Father, Son and Holy Spirit. It is noted that three cups bring good luck, and it is not good to drink only one cup as superstition prevails. Christianity or Coptic Orthodox is practiced in Ethiopia. It is believed the apostle Paul preached in that area.

Creating a fantastic visual image, in the Ethiopian/Eritrean coffee ceremony, the lady of the house usually wearing her colourful garb or wrapped in her white linen shawl, sits on a small stool and has all her utensils set up in front of her on a

*Mehret making Eritrean coffee called Boon
in her traditional Eritrean dress.*

small table. She boils water but first roasts green coffee beans from Ethiopia on a small pan. She chats and laughs and feels completely at ease; masterfully preparing her craft probably having done this coffee ceremony 100 times before. The burnt smell of beans fills the air and after roasting them she passes the blackened beans around on a woven coloured mat so everyone can smell the fresh aroma, smiling and teasing everyone there. People respond with smiles and then wave the smoke-filled aroma three times in front of them.

Like the Indigenous people in Canada in their sweet grass ceremony, the Ethiopians/Eritreans bask the coffee smoke odour three times over themselves on their head, lips and heart as their prayers rise to heaven. Even the youngsters partake in the prayer part although they do not drink the coffee.

Then she grinds the fresh-roasted beans and puts them in a black, clay pot filling it with water and brings it to a boil. Ethiopians/Eritreans are very hospitable people, and love to laugh and joke and share stories. Visitors feel very welcome in

*Mehret putting the roasted beans to boil
for Eritrean coffee in a traditional clay pot.*

Marion Mutala in modern Eritrean/Ethiopian Dress.

their homes as both cultures are proud of their heritage and like to teach others about it. They also like to share their beautiful traditions through many oral stories.

Demi-tasse cups are prepared with sugar or milk or both depending on your preference. They also love their sugar with coffee, and I joke that they have coffee with their sugar not the other way around. The coffee is served on a small matching saucer; popcorn and bread is passed around with the coffee. This coffee ceremony is not rushed and even on Christmas Eve, the children know that presents will not be opened till after the adults have their coffee. One must enjoy and savour the flavour.

When round one is complete, the cups are all collected, washed and ready for cup two followed by round three. It is noted that no more coffee grounds are added to the clay coffee pot, just water. Each time it's brought to a boil, a slow perk, the secret to brewing a fine cup of java. However, the first cup is significantly stronger than cup two or three and can give you a real caffeine buzz, a delicious cup of expresso.

This coffee ceremony takes place in Africa, however the Ethiopians/Eritreans; many who came as refugees to Canada still partake in this practice in their homes in Canada with many friends, relatives and visitors.

There are many cultural experiences in the world to partake like the Japanese Tea Ceremony or the British High Tea. However, if you want to entice your palettes, drop into an Ethiopian/Eritrean home in the late afternoon or evening after supper, to warmly experience a great cuppa boona or boon.

Escape

From 1975-1979 I attended the University of Saskatchewan in Saskatoon, Saskatchewan. When I went to university, I was volunteering with World University Service of Canada (WUSC). In 1977, WUSC started a sponsor-ship refugee program with the University of Saskatchewan to waive tuition fees and room and board for one year and WUSC would provide clothing, books and other miscellaneous daily living expenses. Since the start of this flagship program, other universities in Canada emulated our program. More than 1,000 refugees have come to Canada with this program. The first refugee in this program was named Rezene Tekeste, an Eritrean. On July 20th,1979, I married him, and we had three beautiful children together – my greatest treasures. This is his true story as told to me. I always felt Rezene was like a cat with nine lives as he almost died many times before coming to Canada. It was surprising to me when Rezene died in 2004 of cancer just short of 50 years old.

"Run!" he cried urgently. I did not know his language but understood him, nonetheless. "Run!" I ran as fast as I could and tried to keep up with my nomadic guide leading the way through the trees.

My guide, from a distant tribe, did not speak the same language as me.

I was an Eritrean living in Ethiopia. Tigrinya, my native tongue, is written in a Sabian script, but I also spoke Amharic, the Ethiopian dialect. There are over two hundred dialects and more than 80 tongues in Ethiopia and rural people often speak their own ethnic tongue. But I could tell what my guide was saying – we heard the shots fired at us from soldiers and farmers in the fields. The bullets whizzing by my head.

We both ran, without looking back. I could barely keep up to him. He knew his way in the forest, and it was just beginning to grow dark. I did not want to lose him and followed as close as I could. He was an experienced runner and often helped people escape. For me, I was running for my life. My guide, well, he was running for money.

I fled that day with nothing except the clothes on my back, and one gold cross. I was an Orthodox Christian, and the cross was given to me by my mother, upon my graduation from high school. The decision to leave my beloved homeland of Ethiopia, to leave my mother, my three sisters and one brother, was not an easy one.

I was Eritrean, living in the oldest independent country in Africa known anciently as Abyssinia, or Ethiopia. Eritrea sits on the horn of Africa bordering the Red Sea and Massawa, is a very desirable port; it is one of the world's busiest shipping lanes and the cause of much conflict. The name Eritrea comes from the Greek word "erythrea," meaning red.

In 1974, I was studying second-year medicine in Ethiopia at the University of Haile Selassie and our family lived in Debra Zeit. The government, after the overthrow of Haile Selassie, started killing people and leaving their bodies, dead on their doorsteps.

I did not want my mother, to wake up and find my body on the front steps of her doorway, which was becoming a daily occurrence. My decision to leave was made quickly and secretly. I could not trust anyone as our country was in turmoil. Everyone was extremely suspicious of each other and you could not confide in anyone as the communist regime from 1974 to 1978 was oppressive. People were frightened and uneasy. It was a dark time and there was a huge weight on everyone's shoulders. The period after 1975 became known in history as "Red Terror."

So many people were killed, especially the educated, well-trained, university students – or anyone the communist government deemed to be a threat. The university students were sent out to the depressing countryside. Many were abused, especially girls; they were raped and sometimes became pregnant. It was a terrible situation for women.

In the past, the highest death tolls documented in communist states occurred in the Soviet Union under Joseph Stalin, The Holodomor or "Extermination by Hunger" of Ukrainian people being another, in the People's Republic of China under Mao Zedong, and in Cambodia under the Khmer Rouge. However, there were many mass killings occurring under this regime in Ethiopia at this time. The People's Democratic Republic of Ethiopia who were the government in charge in Ethiopia after Haile Selassie was killed was no better.

Amnesty International estimates that a total of half a million people were killed during the Red Terror of 1977 and 1978. The Save the Children Fund reported that the victims of the Red Terror included not only adults, but 1,000 or more children, mostly aged between 11 and 13.

Mengistu Haile Mariam himself is alleged to have killed political opponents with his bare hands. He was Ethiopia's former ruler and has been convicted of genocide, war crimes and crimes against humanity and sentenced to death by an Ethiopian court for his role in the Red Terror, and the highest-ranking surviving member of the Khmer Rouge has also been charged with those crimes. (*Main article: Red Terror Ethiopia website*)

Emperor Haile Selassie I, the king of Ethiopia, had been a ruler since 1941 and his autocratic ruling created the economic and political turmoil which led to his eventual overthrow in the fall of 1974. When he died a year later, the country was declared a socialist state and the People's Democratic Republic of Ethiopia (PDRE) took over.

"Haile Selassie I (23 July 1892 – 27 August 1975), born Tafari Makonnen Woldemikael, was Ethiopia's regent from 1916 to 1930 and Emperor of Ethiopia from 1930 to 1974. He was the heir to a dynasty that traced its origins by tradition from King Solomon and Queen Makeda, Empress of Axum, known in the Abrahamic tradition as the Queen of Sheba." (*Main article: Red Terror Ethiopia website*)

Many people loved and respected the King; however, he lost touch with his people's needs. Selassie made a major mistake and chose to ignore the plight of many starving people in the north due to drought. There was no food getting through to these people and many were dying. Famine, unemployment and political opposition forced him from office.

This provided the motivation for revolution and a communist government headed by the Marxist dictator Mengistu Haile-Mariam. Mengistu was waiting in the wings for the opportune moment to revolt when Haile Selassie mysteriously died in 1975; in 1977, Mengistu took control as leader of the provisional government.

The new government of the people was backed by the Russian government which was supplying arms to the Ethiopian rebels. There was also a bloody civil war happening with the Eritrean Peoples' Liberation Front (EPLF) which began in 1961 as the Eritreans wanted their freedom and chance to form their own country from Ethiopia. This ongoing battle was relentless and became one of the longest civil wars in the world. The war raged for 35 years before Eritrea became independent.

During the civil war, the Americans supported the Eritreans by sending arms as the government was pro-democracy. Later, in the war, the Russians switched sides and started supporting the Eritreans as the government switched to communism and then tried to liberate them from Ethiopia. In the meantime, the Americans too, switched sides and started helping the Ethiopian government as it was supporting democracy – showing the dirty side and true colour of politics.

The Eritreans did get their freedom and independence in 1993, but the years of conflict created many refugees and many innocent people died. Freedom came with a huge price and life is still not settled in Eritrea under a communist-backed government.

In 1975, under "Red Terror," people were justifiably terrified that they would be the next ones to die and no one could be trusted. The university students protested the coup and the educated people, the first to be killed if they questioned the government, refused to be taken from their studies and sent out to the country to work. They wanted to finish their schooling and contribute to a better society. The government tried to divide and conquer the people.

This was the terror and situation I faced daily and though my decision to leave was a hard one, I thought it better to leave and live than die suddenly. I paid my guide his usual fee of 1000 birr, the Ethiopian currency. Today, that is worth about $46.00 Canadian dollars. We shook hands and I bowed to show respect to an elder. We were both dressed in white cotton traditional garb with white, matching shawls when we left at dusk from Debre-Zeit to head into the desert.

My guide, knowledgeable about crossing the Ogaden desert, knew this dress would help keep us cool as the material breathed, which would manage the heat from the desert during the day, but also provide some warmth at night. The shawl-like scarf would also be used to cover our heads for protection from the direct sunlight like a headdress.

Now running while being shot at, I kept thinking about my mother. I knew how upset she would be, not knowing where I was, thinking perhaps that I was missing or worse yet dead. I knew I had to write to her soon to tell her I was safe.

"That is, if I make it. If the bullets don't kill me first. I must remember to tell my guide to get a message to my mother should anything happen to me. Yes, please, please, please get a message to my mother... another bullet just missed my earlobe."

After what seemed like hours of running through the trees, finally we entered the desert area. I thought, perhaps we would be safe here from humans and guns. Would we? We had different enemies now: the extreme cold at night, combined with the dangerous animals, as well as the extreme heat during the day... besides having no real food other than a bit of bread.

My guide, Amir, spoke again in his Harari dialect. I did not understand his words, but he motioned for us to rest. It was growing dark, so I knew it must be close to six o'clock. Ethiopia was so close to the equator that the sun rose at 6 a.m. and set at 6 p.m. daily, like clockwork. Amir proceeded to make a fire using camel dung. We both slept a fitful and exhausted sleep on the ground. We slept next to the huge fire created for protection from the lions, and for extra warmth of course. The desert gets cold at night.

"Must keep the fire going throughout the night or we will become some animal's supper," I kept thinking as I faded to sleep, too bone-weary to keep my eyes open.

In the morning, we resumed walking and walking and walking. We covered our heads like an East Indian, using the white shawl to create a turban head covering, protection from the hot sun. About midday, we came across a nomadic tribe travelling by camels and luckily, they sold us some milk. We decided to travel with this tribe across the desert. Their diet consisted of camel's milk and bread as we journeyed with them for the next five days.

It did not affect my guide as much as me, he was accustomed to camel's milk… but for me when I was not walking or riding a camel, I was emptying my bowels. My body not used to the rich camel's milk was racked with huge bouts of diarrhea.

Camels are ornery beasts – aggressive in nature and they get mad easily. They can be quite dangerous if you do not know how to handle them, so I was glad when we departed and headed in a different direction from the tribe.

Exhausted from the oppressive heat during the day and extreme cold at night, we curled up close to the fire each night. We were always aware that if our fire went out, we were at risk of being a midnight snack to the hyenas that prowled around our campfire noisily; their creepy laughing caused the hair on my arms to stand on end. We desperately kept the camel dung burning high.

On day seven, we reached a border crossing. I was not sure where but believe that it might have been the Yabelo or Haran border. There were soldiers at the crossing, and they started to interrogate me.

"Where are you going? Why are you crossing here?" The soldiers wanted us to go back. They had enough of refugees.

Luckily, my guide knew the soldiers and crossed here regularly. He was able to sweet-talk, bribe them, so they willingly let me cross into their country, Somalia. I said goodbye to my guide and hugged him with the usual Eritrean custom of touching shoulders, shaking hands and kissing each cheek three times.

Was this a kiss of death? I hoped not. The guards took me to a refugee camp by the Indian Ocean situated near the outskirts of the capital city, Mogadishu. By this time, I was feeling extremely sick. I was dehydrated, had a high fever and had lost a lot of weight. When I reached the refugee camp I fainted. The doctor took one look at me and put me on an IV. I was too ill to eat, and the doctor thought he should build up my immune system. He proceeded to insert iron into my IV bag. Immediately, I could feel my body tighten up, swelling rapidly.

"Deehhhh!" I shouted, half asleep. "What is happening?" My eyelids, my cheeks, my lips, my entire face was ballooning; my fingers, my hands, my arms, my ankles, my toes, my feet, my whole body was swelling and swelling and swelling. I started yelling again, "Deehhhh!"

I grabbed the IV needle from my arm and pulled it out. "No, no, no!" I screamed loudly in Tigrinya. "I am allergic to iron." Having studied medicine for the past two years, I knew this. Plus, I had had a similar experience before.

"Iron, allergic to iron. Do not give me iron," I shouted, half in English and half in Tigrinya. The nurses and doctors looked at me as if I was losing my mind.

Finally, I made them understand what was wrong. I was down to 38.5 kilograms and had a high fever. Luck was with me again, life number four, having escaped being shot at by farmers, one week's crossing the desert and hyenas and lions at night. I stayed in the refugee hospital for a month before I recovered sufficiently to leave, my strength and energy so depleted from my desert crossing. The doctors also determined I had malaria and were giving me penicillin.

Once I had regained a little strength, I immediately wrote a letter to my mother telling her I was alive and well. No use to worry her. I could only imagine what hell she was going through not having heard from me these past two months.

When the other refugees in the camp saw I could read and

write, I became a reader, a translator and a letter writer for them. This helped me survive. Many of the other refugees were illiterate, so they would get me to write or read their letters. They'd pay me with extra food, a few coins or items of clothing.

Many wanted to contact their families, so I was kept busy. This helped pass the time as boredom could kill you as well. More importantly, this raised my status in the camp and helped protect me. I could trade my skills for food, water, soap, blankets and anything else I needed to get by.

One of the refugees could tell I was still not well and brought me onions to eat as he thought this would help build my strength. It worked and I started to feel better. I knew I needed to plan my future and it was not in this refugee camp in Somalia. There was no hope or future here. The Somalis had their own problems; did not want us in their country and were at war with the Ethiopians. People became stuck in refugee camps for years; often never left. I needed to get out fast while I was still able to move. The camp was set up near the water and I began to plan my next escape.

I started inquiring secretively about how I could leave. I asked lots of questions to different people about surrounding countries, pretending to study and was simply curious. I pored over a map to pick the safest route. I would tell no one of my plan – like last time – I could not really trust anyone. Being in a refugee camp does not mean you are safe or fed. It really is survival of the fittest; there were rapes, attacks, intimidation, extortion and death in the camps. The longer I stayed, the more desperate I was to leave. My plan was just to ask innocent questions, so no one became suspicious. My next escape would be planned, but sudden as well.

My plan was to take a boat to Kenya, the neighbouring country. The refugee camp was located close to the Indian

Ocean and what better or faster way to travel than by boat. Surely, it would be safer than crossing the desert on foot or by camel. I had had enough of the extreme heat and the cold and the constant worry of animals at night from my desert crossing.

Had I known the odds of making it by water, had I heard the stories of bodies being tossed overboard, of people dying while being smuggled into countries, of the Vietnamese Boat People tragedy that was on the news, or Syrian refugees today, I might have come up with a different plan. But I knew nothing of such dangers and proceeded with my idea.

I had some cash saved up from translating. I met with a man who delivered goods to the refugee camp and he had a small vessel and agreed to take me to Kenya. We would enter at the port of Mombasa as he had friends that were guards there and could help us with a safe entry. We agreed to leave at night, when it was dark and most people were sleeping, so no one would see us or try to stop us. I told no one else I was leaving.

I did not have to worry about packing any bags or luggage. I had the clothes on my back, an extra sweater and shawl for warmth, my gold cross, and some American money which I had gotten on the black market in exchange for my Ethiopian birr. The boat captain wanted cold American cash.

Ethiopian birr or Somalian shillings would be useless in Kenya anyway, as they had their own shilling. I also carried some bottled water in my shawl, along with an Eritrean bread called hambasha – it is flat, slightly leavened, and very tasty.

My stomach was fluttering from nerves when I climbed on to the boat. I had never been on a boat before and felt I might be sick. I did not know this man from Adam. "Ali" was a Somalian trying to make a living any way he could and had five other refugees, all men, trying to escape like me on his cargo boat.

We had to stay hidden from sight as we were illegal cargo.

Caught, Ali could be put in jail for transporting humans. I agreed to pay him $100 American but did not want to give it all to him in advance. I thought it would be better to give $50 upfront and $50 when we arrived in Kenya. However, Ali was a smart businessman and would not let me step onto the boat unless he had all the money in hand. No doubt, his concern was whether I did indeed have the full amount. No money, no passage.

Trust… what makes a man trust another? I had no choice. Plus, it was only money – what good would money do if I was dead? I needed to survive for my mother's sake. I could picture her giving me the gold, Orthodox cross for my graduation. She was dressed in her Eritrean clothes, the shawl covering the left side of her face where she had a scar and was partially paralyzed, perhaps because of a stroke or Bell's Palsy. She looked happy and proud and was ululating loudly. This is a guttural sound of joy; women make at the back of their throat in celebration.

I fingered the cross and said a silent prayer: "Please, please, please, God help me!"

"Mother, please be with me on this journey. I need to see your face again."

The journey was uneventful and though we were terrified, we slept on and off fitfully during the entire trip. None of us spoke while we shared this journey of silence and fear. Our body language said it all. The trip could take up to five days, but the captain hoped to do it in three days if we were very lucky and God or Allah was with us.

It was risky business and the boat travelled slowly, as close to shore as possible; the captain was constantly on the lookout for pirates, thieves or boat border patrols checking for illegal passengers. The entire trip was roughly 441 kilometres. The

Indian Ocean or sea could be rough at times, especially during the months of July and August, but we were travelling during October, which has a seasonal wind shift, and, in the summer, it has heavy rains during the monsoon season, but during fall it is very hot and dry. God must have been with us for just as the sun was rising on the third day, we entered a port area in Kenya.

As we disembarked from the boat, I realized how lucky, again, I was to survive the trip. My legs were cramped and stiff from the crowded space. I had been scared out of my wits for the past three days. Filled with emotion I thanked God, and the captain as well. I shook his hand, then hugged him with tears running down my cheeks. He said "Salem, peace be with you" the usual greeting for he was Muslim and so was his Muslim soldier friend we met at the border crossing on arrival in Kenya.

The Muslim guard saw my cross and said, "Are you a Christian?" I was scared to answer him as sometimes there is conflict between Muslims and Christians. Yet, I could not deny that I was Christian as I was wearing a gold cross and he saw it. Why else would I be wearing a gold cross? "Yes," I said quietly in English.

Suddenly, I fainted. The Muslim soldier caught me. The next thing I knew, I woke up in a strange room. I was being looked after by this soldier. He said I had slept for 48 hours straight. He was preparing some food and said I needed to eat some liver and onions. The Muslim guard had taken me in his truck to his home in Nairobi, but I was totally unaware of the two-day journey.

This man was like my guardian angel. He nursed me. I was very sick – perhaps my malaria had come back – so Mohamed, this soldier, let me stay with him until I got well. I believe I was there a week, not sure of the time or day anymore, my fever at times making me delirious. I slept, ate and dreamt, tossing from frequent nightmares of being shot. Mohamed was a very patient man, soft spoken and gentle.

He wanted to feed me liver and onions chopped and ground up fine, very well cooked. I do not know why, to this day, the food did not make me sick, although liver is very high in iron. He fed me so much liver and onions that finally, one day, my fever broke. I could feel myself start to heal.

It seemed to help enormously. Feeling better, after another three days, I knew I had to make my own way in this world. This kind man, this stranger, was putting his life in danger and could get into big trouble as he was a guard and soldier. He might lose his job or be put in jail for helping an illegal immigrant. He risked his life for me. I will be eternally grateful to him.

I offered him the rest of my money, $10 American. He refused and quoted the Koran, a passage about "saving a man's life, save the world." However, I left it secretly on the table. Mohamed had indeed saved my life; again, life number seven and I was very thankful. "Thanks be to God and Mohamed," I prayed and hugged him. He smiled and said, "May Allah be with you."

I headed out towards the urban refugee camp in Nairobi. Mohamed pointed me in the right direction, gave me water and food, and I ventured out into the unknown abyss. After walking for what seemed like hours, I began to grow weary. It was growing dark rapidly, my walking was so slow, and I was still very tired. I found an old, abandoned shed to sleep in. I thought I would sleep here the night and arrive at the refugee camp in the morning.

I must have passed out from fatigue, as I do not remember anything for the next few hours. Suddenly, I awoke with a start. Someone was pawing and grabbing me. A man was trying to rob me. I saw a knife flash and knew he was going to stab me, perhaps kill me. I rolled over quickly, jumped up, and high tailed it out of that shed not looking back at my attacker. I left my shawl along with the little bit of food and water, and I just ran and ran and ran, my heart pounding in my chest. I ran and wept, and then ran some more. I ran like a rabbit until I could not run anymore.

My legs were spent. "What is going on?" I thought. "Will the danger never end?" I was sobbing while trying to catch my breath, and as I was running, I became extremely upset. I had reached my wit's end and I cried to God aloud just like Job did in the Bible.

"What am I to do? Where am I to go? Where will I be safe?" What did God want from me? I questioned and demanded answers. I had had enough and had reached my breaking point.

After what seemed like hours, but must have been only minutes, I finally stopped running and tried to calm down. Suddenly, there seemed to be a great many people around and lots of activity. It was daylight. I listened and looked for a sign, a person that could help, or something familiar. I needed to find a haven. Was that possible for a sick, Eritrean refugee running from Ethiopia to Somalia and now into another strange African country?

Between the Kenyan, Swahili dialect and people greeting each other with "Jambo," Nairobi quickly came to life. Later, in my life, I discovered Nairobi to Africans, was like Hawaii to North Americans – a great destination point. On this morning the noise, hustle, and bustle of a large city boomed in my ears. Music was blasting, with heavy traffic flowing. I never had time to process what really happened to me in that shed and was too scared to think about it. Did someone really try to rob and stab me to death?

I could not even go there, my mind in such a daze. I was

feeling stunned. I wandered around aimlessly, moving up and down streets, my body feeling like it was dreaming or in a trance. I felt hallucinatory - maybe from lack of food, water or perhaps my fever had come back.

Seconds turned to minutes; minutes turned to hours. My mind kept saying, "Keep going, don't stop moving," my legs walked aimlessly, without direction. What was I to do? Where was I to go? Frustrated and drained, I sat down on the street curb and put my face in my hands.

"What was that?" I thought I heard some Tigrinya, my native tongue, spoken through the commotion and confusion. "Really? What is that? Where is that sound coming from?"

Thinking I was probably nuts or perhaps dreaming, I listened more closely. It was a magnificent song to my foreign ears.

I followed the musicality of my language and ran up to a group of people shouting, "Kamay, Kamay, aloha. How are you?" I repeated myself over and over. Though strangers to me, they were my newfound friends and I greeted them happily in the traditional, Eritrean way of shaking hands while touching shoulders and cheeks together. I was ecstatic.

They were surprised to see me so excited and wondered what was going on. Perhaps, I looked like a madman from hell, all disheveled and out of sorts. I started to cry, tears of joy, and the group of men hushed me and said, "Naaa, naaa, come, come with us." The three Eritrean men – refugees, like me – took me to the urban refugee camp I was looking for in Kenya. This camp would become my home for the next two years. These people would become my new family.

Laughing and crying all at once, I started talking faster and faster and tried to explain my story repeatedly. They understood my concern and tried to calm me. They made me some spiced tea with cardamom, cloves, cinnamon bark, milk and sugar - just like back home. They also gave me some bread to eat; delicious, beautiful, hambasha.

When I think back on my life, I will always remember that special moment: that tea, that bread, that feeling of finding my own people again and speaking my native tongue. They were strangers but they were like best friends for I was lost and had been found and needed them more than ever in this vulnerable state. It had been almost one year since I'd escaped from Ethiopia and started my journey as a refugee. I was home. Well, it sure felt like it anyway. For now, ...

Living in that camp was one of the happiest times I had ever experienced as a homeless, stateless person in my newly found status as a refugee. To this day, I still remember feeling a strange calmness come over my body, a feeling of belonging, a feeling of home, a feeling of being in God's arms. "Will I be safe now?" I wondered. Temporarily, maybe...

Traditional Eritrean Doro Wat- a Berbere hot sauce and Injera rolled flat pancake that you open and put the sauce on top and eat with your hands.

The Obsession

We lived in our dream home. 10 acres of prime property located south of Saskatoon. My husband and I drove for months searching and waiting for the perfect place. Friends laughed when seeing the two-headed driver in the 57 Chevy truck. "Honeymooners," they said. "Don't worry give it a year or two it will change." We were recently married and madly in love. Joe, my husband was Twitter pated like the skunk in Bambi. I was the perfect wife having found my soul mate and mated for life.

That was five years ago.

Today, living in a magnificent, scenic log cabin, built from our sweat labour, we were so content. Nothing could ruin our plans of a peaceful, quiet, early retirement lifestyle in our natural setting. How wrong we were!

Unexpectedly, after living together, we discovered certain items out of place or missing. Small items at first, then larger ones and more personal things like my writings. I felt invaded and constantly watched. Truthfully, my husband and I were just plain scared.

At first, we blamed the other. "Joe, were you reading my diary? I can't find it. Where did you put it?" I screamed at him. Or on planning a romantic evening Joe inquired, "Where is that candelabra, I gave you on our wedding day? What did you do sell it?" Joe yelled at me.

The tension escalated and we argued more frequently. A

missing wedding band, missing wedding photos, and a missing negligee - this was getting personal.

Then the compulsion became obsessive. We both needed to find who or what was driving us apart and seizing our things - our very personal belongings. We planted traps, planned strategies to attack, and became more frustrated with fruitless results! Our dream home suddenly became a prison, entrapping, yet disclosing no helpful information. I felt Joe was no longer my soul mate and his twitter pated state had dissipated through the strain. We were at wits end and ready to call it quits.

Joe was placing the "For Sale" sign on our lawn the day I noticed. Through the trees, I glimpsed someone peeking. Following… carefully 10 paces behind, not wanting to lose sight; yet not wanting to become discovered I hurried after him. Pursuing through large bushes and steep paths, I was finally led to this huge hill in the backwoods of our property.

Funny, in five years, I had not been back to that old cabin at the back of our property as we were so focused on building our dream home. I continued over that hill, down a ravine leading to that old place beside a sparkling, brook. It was no longer old but was now someone else's dream paradise! Amazingly, it had been recreated to parallel our new log house. Well-kept and immaculately maintained, it resembled our present dwelling.

For a moment, so taken by the scene, I completely forgot where or why I was here.

Entering through a familiar door, walking on exact hardwood flooring, into a gigantic sun-filled solarium with a fireplace, I was lost and shocked.

Inside was our missing paraphernalia from the past years. On the front table, was our beautifully, carved, mahogany wedding candelabra. Often, I had wondered what happened to that special present given to me by my husband on our special day.

Climbing the spiraling stairs, leading to our loft-like bedroom something surprised me – but only for a minute. Perceiving I had been here before, somewhere in my dreams, I recognized the eyes and remembered the face. On the bed, ahead were the sparkling, sad eyes belonging to the man who had lost his wife and was forced to sell his dream property to pay for his wife's medical bills or so he had explained.

I remember how sad he was at the thought of having to sell all 10 acres of land. I believe his wife and him had just bought the property and were planning to build when she became sick. I had no idea he recreated their dream home and planted it where their old house had been. What a shock!

Looking into this man's eyes, I witnessed his previous passion and forlorn grief. I was no longer afraid. This man had dreams equal to ours and tried to live them out here alone, in his dream cabin, his late wife's and his dream cabin. This man sold us his dream five years ago when his wife died.

Walking quietly home, towards my dream and log haven I ran in to disclose my enlightenment and discovery to my husband, Joe my soul mate.

"Joe, guess what. Come with me," I cried. "I have something important to show you."

Intrigued but worried Joe followed along.

"Where are we going, he asked curiously? I need to know."

"Just you wait and see. I have a pleasant surprise for you."

Joe was as shocked as I was when I showed him the log cabin.

Joe said, "Let's go meet him and talk with him and assure him he can stay if he wants."

"If he returns our items, he borrowed." I sighed. "Those are precious reminders of our life."

"I am sure he will when we explain." replied Joe.

Joe and our new neighbour Bill became fast friends. He returned our items and we never missed another thing. We finally felt safe knowing Bill was watching over us.

Taking down the "For Sale" from our front lawn I knew deep in my heart, this man's dream and secret would always be safe with us!

But Diamonds are a Girl's Best Friend

"Sold to the fellow in the second row – she's an eight, she's a nine, and she's a ten you know."

I was singing along with my iPod to John Michael Montgomery's song. I loved that song. "And I'm about to bid my heart goodbye" blaring along with the music blasting the room. Secretly, I wondered if guys fell head over heels the way girls do or as their music sometimes portrays.

"Oh, I wish I could have a guy say those words to me." I wailed. "Susie you are so lucky, you have fallen in love and Randy's so cute."

We were lying in bed planning and dreaming about Susie's wedding next summer. "Look at this great wedding dress and only five grand." squealed Susie as she paged through the latest Vogue. Susie's parents did not have the money to plan an expensive wedding, but of course they gave Susie everything she wanted, as she was an only girl.

"You're so lucky Susie. You never have to wear hand-me downs." I was the ninth in my family and lived on second-hand clothes. "Your parents will buy you anything and your wedding day will be so special." I voiced jealously.

"We are having six attendants, two flower girls, two ring boys, a huge five-layered tiered cake with sequins and the wedding will be at Bessborough Gardens." Susie exclaimed out of breath.

"How much is that a plate?" I asked, always the practical person.

"We don't buy the plate Marion," Susie chirped.

"No, I mean per person. How much does it cost to eat there for each person?" knowing she had invited 200 guests.

Rolling my eyes, I tried to explain this to my best friend since grade school, but sometimes...

"MARION, DO YOU THINK I KNOW OR CARE?" she professed.

"This is my special day and my parents said I could have whatever I wanted. I don't worry about money. That will be Randy's job when we get married. I get to stay home and be a housewife. He promised me that already and we are going to have a huge house in Greenbryre with all new furniture. My own paradise for Randy and me to live happily together, forever. I get to stay home, sleep in and watch the afternoon soaps."

"Don't you want to get a career or aspire to be or do something?"

Secretly, I was an aspiring author.

"Don't you have dreams?"

"Yes of course I do. Randy and I will live happily ever after; he will be at my beck and call and buy me whatever I want. I am getting a mink coat for our first anniversary. Isn't that glorious?"

Susie was so unbelievable sometimes. All she did was dream about material things. It was hard to believe we were still friends, after all these years. I came from a hard-working, farming family of 12 and she lived in the city with one brother. We became neighbours and attended the same school when my family sold the farm after my dad retired and moved to Saskatoon, Saskatchewan.

Her mom had monthly manicures and a weekly hairdo and sipped on Martinis. She never cooked. My mom baked bread, baked pies, and made delicious preserves. Their family ordered in Pizza and Chinese whenever and I envied her lifestyle but was worried for her as well. This was the 21st century and women worked, had careers and the divorce rate was 50%.

I could spell trouble already, but I did not want to puncture her balloon. It seemed Susie was selling her soul for her Wedding Day. Waving her one carat diamond engagement ring around, Susie tossed back her long, blonde hair and proceeded to talk about Randy's cute butt. Switching from the iPod to laptop we zoomed through the sites and glanced at Marilyn Monroe singing her famous song, "But Diamonds Are a Girl's Best Friend."

"Isn't she gorgeous?" says Susie. "I want to be just like her and have all that beautiful jewellery. Diamonds are the best things, Marion. Make sure when you get engaged, your man buys the biggest ring in the store because that tells the world how much he really loves you. See how huge my diamond ring is? Randy loves me a lot."

Randy, should we talk about Randy now? Cute butt and all… No let's not go there, I said to myself as I thought about Marilyn's early demise.

Hanky Panky

"Surely there must have been something going on," I questioned Bill rudely.

"No," he said, "not that I know of."

"Come on now, Bill there must have been some "hanky panky."

"Imagine, two brothers living in the same house, George and Peter and George's wife, Sally and three bedrooms. Sounds like a love triangle to me." I laughed aloud.

Bill only smiled slightly, not wanting to think about why his uncle who never married lived with his mom and dad and family on the farm.

"How do you think she had all those children? It might have been common, as Catholics to have so many children. The Priest preached it from the pulpit. Go forth and multiply. But 14 children for a British family, during the depression was rare. The British seemed to have the "in" on birth control.

Bill smiled and said, "That is why there were three bedrooms on the main floor. I slept with my uncle growing up and mom and dad had their own bedroom. Birth control."

"Well, it didn't work very well, 14 children, 14 live births. Four died as infants. But still 14 pregnancies and no twins. All single births. Your mom must have been pregnant her whole adult life."

"Yeah, and she was only a half pint, barely 1.52 metres, more like 1.47 metres, a small delicate, frail woman, all-natural births and some of them born right at home."

"Well, tell me more about this love triangle?" me not wanting to change the subject.

"Your mom must have had the perfect set up. When she was sick of one guy she could hook up with the brother. Why do you think your Uncle Peter never married?"

"Never met the right lady. He never was engaged... not that I remember or know. Hey, I never asked him. I minded my own business like you should. You ask way too many questions," he said a little embarrassed.

No one wants to think their parents cheat. No one wants to think that his Uncle and his mom were having "coochee coo" on the side.

"You are pretty disrespectful." Bill snarls at me.

"I thought we are such good friends, and we can talk about anything," I say.

I could tell Bill had enough for one day. I tried one last pitch, "What was their relationship like?"

"My dad and Uncle farmed together. My uncle was a better farmer than dad and he was more organized and reliable. My dad would go for coffee or to the bar with his friends all the time and Uncle Peter would get the crops in on time, buy a new combine and maintain the working machinery. He even helped pay the bills, the phone, and electricity, buy food; if it wasn't for him, we would have had it pretty rough at times. But because he helped out life was easier for us – especially with 10 surviving children."

Not wanting to upset my good friend anymore; he was feeling rather uncomfortable, I suggested we look at some old photographs of his family. He proceeded to tell me his mom and dad had eloped at the age of 16 without parental consent.

"Wow! What wild parents you had – to run away and elope." I declared.

"I was very close to my Uncle and I use to help him farm when I was young. I would hang out with him and sleep at his feet on the tractor. He taught me lots of stuff and I was closer to him than my dad. He was awesome. When I was older, I bought his farmland from him and took over the family farm. My brothers and sisters were always jealous of our relationship, but I worked hard and listened to Uncle Peter. He gave good advice and was easy to talk to."

"Sounds like he was like a father-figure to you."

"Yeah, he was. He was more of a father than my own father. Here is a picture of him. This is my Uncle Peter." He showed me the worn black and white photograph dated 1930.

"He never married. Hey, no girlfriends, no broken engagements?" I asked.

"Not that I know of," Bill said angrily, having been questioned enough.

"Well, he sure was a looker." I smiled quietly to myself.

I really should keep my mouth shut, sometimes. That picture sure looked a lot like Bill. I smiled to myself again. Genetics sure are funny, I thought to myself. Bill looks more like his Uncle then his dad.

"No hanky panky, suurre, hey." Lol. I think to myself.

"Not!"

He's Hot

"You are not really going to do this are you?"

"Why not?"

"Well to start, how about because it is unethical, immoral, deceitful that's why?"

"So?"

"I'm your best friend. I am advising you not to do this nasty deed."

"Listen Marion, have I ever listened to you before?"

I shook my head in agreement, knowing full well, she was one stubborn cookie. What Kate wants; Kate gets. Arguing with her was fruitless.

"I know just the person I want too. There he is."

"Where?"

"Over by the bar."

"He has sucker written all over his face. I am going to take him for the ride of his life, tonight. Yeah, a costly ride at that." Kate sounded heartless.

"Kate do not do this," I say. "I have fear in my heart for you. This cannot be good for you."

"Look at his face; he's gorgeous, blonde, blue eyes, good genes. Look at his designer clothes and he was driving a Lamborghini. He reeks of money."

"Deception is never good," I say. "This is just plain evil."

With keys in my hand, I had a very sick feeling about this

whole thing. Should I tell him about her plan? SHOULD I EXPOSE HER DECEIT?

I was her best friend. Yet, I wondered about that at this moment. How could we still be best friends with such different morals? My stomach was turning, and it was not from all the alcohol I had consumed.

The blonde guy was in for some heat alright. He was hot, alright, a hot man, but his world was about to change forever. I glanced over at Kate flirting with this man at the bar.

Kate, my best friend since elementary school, 29-year-old, fertile Kate. Ripe as ever, looking for a man to impregnate her and support her. Her biological clock was ticking away.

"A life sentence," I thought to myself, "happening to one hot man," as Kate and her hunk walked out the door together, holding hands and kissing passionately.

Well, of course you want to know what happened to Kate and her story. She did become pregnant and had a baby but not with this rich guy. When they left the bar together, the rich guy became suspicious when Kate asked him to buy her a diamond ring displayed in the window as they walked by. He was on to her and he dumped her before they even got to the car.

Kate was so mad she picked up the first guy she saw at the bar and had sex and yes, she was fertile. Of course, the guy was poor and wanted nothing to do with her again. Poor Kate. Now single, pregnant and foiled at her own game with no diamond on her finger.

One Simple Glance

She glanced at him and he glanced at her. It was a quick glance, but their eyes met and held for a second, not a long second, not a long glance, but it was magical. One simple moment in time, one simple glance, one millisecond, but that glance changed everything.

And, if I had not paid attention, observed that precious moment, I would not have known. I would have missed it completely. Yes, they sat in front of me, I was watching, I was observing. I did notice. Yes, it was there, that simple glance and millisecond in time and now I know why.

My girlfriend, a writer, once told me when something bad happens, after the stuff hits the fan literally…when all is said and done, you should pause, laugh and then say, "Hey, more good writing material."

I am not sure I can be so realistic or laughable about my life, as I have had some real stinky stuff happen to me. Some of it wasn't funny or even laughable.

However, I will give her credit for one idea. It does help to write about it. Venting on paper brings great satisfaction. I remember after a certain tragic incident, being so upset that I typed for five hours straight. It was writing material and it sure helped to spill it out onto paper. Whether it was publishable material or not didn't matter at this point. Therapeutic writing.

Another strategy, she suggested was keeping a journal.

Watch people use your powers of observation and take notes. That suggestion was nothing new.

I was a born people watcher, a good listener and must have a trusting face because people have told me some pretty sketchy stuff, sad tales and weird things claiming to be true. To me, I simply say, TMI, "Too much information." Please don't share that.

Lately, I have been watching people closer and writing about my observations. Single again, I have been checking out available men. For example, there is this one guy I know and am rather interested in and we have frequently ended up at the same events.

Just the other evening, we were both at a gala wine and cheese party that was kind of fun. He was there and I was there. I thought tonight, I should make my move. So, I was sitting at the table behind him, observing from afar like I normally do, enjoying my solitary wine and brie cheese. This man was a true gentleman, a handsome face, though balding, but tall and in good shape and seemingly available. I was more than kind of interested in him.

While I was checking him out, I went through the previous data I had collected on him. Single, white male never married, no children, 55 years old, wealthy, university educated, white collar worker, unattached and kind. I knew he had been engaged twice before, but both times he was rejected, one lady left him alone at the altar and the other one cheated on him with his best friend. From my data collection, I rationalized facts to narrow my odds to find a lasting relationship.

These questions played out in my mind.

Is he a player or ladies' man?

Is he gay?

Is he a man of the cloth, priestly in character, married to Christ perhaps?

Is he a drug addict, a drunk, weirdo, with disgusting habits that makes him undesirable?

Is he unemployed?

Is he a mama's boy?

Is he egocentric or just plain annoying?

Is he a smoker?

Did I cover all the bases? These were all very important questions.

I chuckled to myself. Now, before I have certain human rights groups on my back, let it be known, a woman has an inalienable right and need to check out all these factors before she starts pursuing any man. One must be safe, and one has a right to be selective. Certainly, it is in the Female's Charter when seeking a mate to have unspeakable human rights.

Let us call him, my potential mate, Stan. Well Stan, in my opinion was a sure thing, the real McCoy, the bases were loaded in my favour and believed I could hit a homerun with Stan. Stan was sitting at a table with two other ladies and a gentleman. The one lady was with her husband, an older couple, so Stan was clearly not with them. The other lady was a 55ish, distinguished, quite elegantly dressed, professional career woman but it was a well-known fact that she was married, and her husband was home sick that night.

So, given my first opportunity, I thought, I would make my move. Stan was just chatting away harmlessly at the table, having a glass of the good stuff, idly visiting and making small talk. Now remember, this is when a writer's keen sense of observation comes into play.

I almost missed it. It happened so quickly. I would not have noticed, if my eyes were not stalking him. It happened at the table, when they both got up to get more wine. The table, where he was sitting, was directly in front of me. Stan, the supposed eligible bachelor… the man I was going to hit a homerun, spoiled my game plan.

Before, I had a chance to make my move, all four of them got up at the same time, as if it was planned. Luckily, the older lady in my sight was short; otherwise, I might have missed it. As the people at the table in front of us, leaned in to pick up their wine glasses for refills, the other married lady, whose husband was home sick, leaned forward slightly, innocently towards Stan, to pick up her wine glass.

At that exact moment as if on cue, so did Stan. They moved closer towards each other to say a few words. She leans in real close to say something to Stan, but as she does, they almost touch foreheads, almost brush lips, almost kiss, but not quite, as it happened fast. No one would have noticed. They did not touch, or kiss, but her leaning, matched his leaning.

Stan copied her gestures, forward, almost brushing foreheads, almost a lip brush. Their eyes locked in place; not long, but long enough. And there it was, that millisecond of observation that glance, one simple glance.

"Eureka," I shockingly exclaimed to myself, that is why he is not married. That is why single Stan, my Stan, my perfect match and homerun Stan, is still single. I guess, I did not weigh all the options, cover all the bases, nor ask the right questions. There will be no homerun for me tonight.

Mmm, a married woman, an eligible, attractive bachelor. I'm slipping. That scenario was the oldest scenario, older than prostitution. It did not cross my mind, and me, a professional writer. What was I thinking?

She glanced at him and he glanced at her. It was a quick glance, but their eyes met and held for a second, not a long second, not a long glance, but it was magical. One simple moment in time, one simple glance, one millisecond, but, that glance changed everything. And, if I had not paid attention, observed that precious moment, I would not have known. I would have missed it completely.

Yes, they sat in front of me, I was watching, I was observing. I did notice. I was paying attention, I noticed. I know why that eligible bachelor Stan, my perfect mate, is not eligible.

Who would have thunk that he was the type to be gallivanting around with a married woman?

BFF

"The times they were changing" ... Bob Dylan sang on the radio and we sang along with him. Me and Sandi, Sandi and me. We were inseparable. We could have been twins. We liked the same music, the same food, and the same clothes. We dressed the same; cut our blonde hair the same. People even said we looked the same. We had known each other since grade one. It would have been kindergarten, but there was no kindergarten in those days in small town, Saskatchewan at Star School.

Our desks were across from each other, every recess we hung out on the playground and at lunch time, we sat and ate our lunches together as we were lunch pals. We even rode on the same school bus together, sat in same seat for 12 years. When we were in grade five, we were allowed sleepovers and from that day forward we became inseparable. Alternating back and forth from Sandi's house to my house every weekend and we began to call each others parent's mom and dad.

Yes, we would have been BFF, Best Friends Forever, if that phrase had been coined in the late 60's or early 70's. We were best friends. When we went to the Saskatoon exhibition in grade eight, we found a necklace and had each of our names engraved in a circle and then split in half. Sandi and I divided one half of our name, and each wore the other half of the person's name on one chain enclosed in that golden circled necklace. I wore the San of Sandi and she wore the Kim of Kimberly.

In grade nine, at the start of high school, a time when girlfriends find other girlfriends, we pinky swore, pinched our fingers with needles, until blood squirted out and then mixed our blood together and became blood sisters. That was the day before aids or STD'S and the start of the "make love, not war revolution."

It was the start of the hippie movement in the States but in Saskatchewan, not many hippies were around, and we were too young to attend Woodstock born in 1957, the tail end of the baby boomers.

Upon graduation from high school, we both decided to move to the big city of Saskatoon, Saskatchewan and became roomies. We took the same secretarial course and still dressed and ate the same. We even double dated as double dating was common in those days and our boyfriends even looked the same and had been our high school sweethearts.

What can I say BFF? Best Friends Forever…

Marrying our childhood sweethearts was no surprise to either of our families and buying houses in the same neighbourhood, on the same block, not unheard of either.

I mean that is what best friends do. We still talked every day, kept in touch, coiffed together, became pregnant at the same time, and raised kids together, having our first boys born, the same month. Unbelievable maybe, but we were hopeful our children would become BFF, especially when we both had girls, a week apart and I named my daughter Sandi and Sandi named her daughter Kimberley, after me. Why not?

BFF was everything. Even our hubbies hung out together and became BFF if men do that kind of thing. Why not share everything? Life was good and we were so happy.

So perhaps, I should not have been surprised when it

happened. I should not have even been fazed by it. BFF shared everything, did they not? We knew everything about each other, and our schedules coincided so that we babysat for each other.

When I had to go to my doctor's appointment for a pregnancy test confirming I was once again pregnant, it should have been the first warning sign, as Sandi was not pregnant; even though, her husband and her had tried for another child. I was glowing and happy at the idea of having another child, but hesitant to be so happy, to cause any pain for my BFF, Sandi.

My appointment was for one pm and when I got there, I found out that my appointment had been rescheduled, as my doctor was called to an emergency at the hospital. Our doctor, Sandi and my doctor's cancellation was a total surprise. That had never happened before. I guess that should have been the second warning sign that things were out of kilter. My baby moved a bit inside, and my stomach felt queasy.

How was she to know? How was he to know? Sandi, my husband; how were they to know that my appointment was rescheduled, and I would be home early and would walk into my own house, into my own bedroom, and see them in my own bed.

So why was I so shocked, when I walked in on them? My husband and my BF forever... the split half necklace we shared, still wore with the "San" attached to the "berly" mixed on my chain and Sandi, my best friend forever, still wearing the "Kim" and "di" part mixed together on her chain around her neck, quite visible as I walked in, around her naked neck.

The necklace was there for a reason was it not? A sign, a symbolic reminder of BFF. Best Friends Forever!

Secrets

Can you keep a secret? This opens ears wide as Niagara Falls. Two secrets. A Baby and Accident. Nothing though, is what it seems.

I was working in a nursing home for the summer as a university student and could not believe how the employees use to love watching their soaps. I had watched a bit with the workers but as a naive 19-year-old girl thought the soaps were ridiculous. Those things do not happen.

Fast forward 40 years. Those soaps were tame compared to some people's lives.

Story 1
A Baby

It is unbelievable how a school reunion can change two entire families' lives. A hook-up of high school sweethearts. If society had been different in the early 70's maybe this might not have happened.

"Two roads and I took the one less travelled by," says Frost.

We all have a road or choices we make in life. One decision can affect you forever.

The year 2000 – a 25-year school reunion.

"Can you believe it we have been out of school for 25 years already?" says Julie.

"What have we done with our lives?" says Bob. 25 classmates – three deceased, Sam, Tom and Lily, cancer, car accident and heart problems.

"I wonder if Jim will be here." interjects Julie.

"Oh yes," says Nick. "He is coming."

"I haven't seen him since we graduated in 1973. It will be great to see him again." remarks Julie.

"Weren't you dating?" murmurs Bill.

"Yeah, well he was sure cute and quite a hunk. I can hardly wait to see him again."

At that moment Jim walks in the door and Julie is embarrassed.

The reunion was quite the party with a barbecue, dance and wiener roast. A three-day bash can change your life.

"Jim and Julie connected again as if they had unfinished business." said Marg.

"I guess they have unfinished business," said Vivian.

"What do you mean?" I said.

"You never heard?" I was the last to hear gossip.

"After the reunion everyone went back to their prospective life. Julie and Jim divorced their partners and got married."

"What?" I said, "How did that happen?"

"You know the reunion last year they were all over each other. Well, that was not just a three-day fling. They really did have unfinished business. Really." said Vivian.

"Apparently they are looking for their daughter together."

"Daughter," I said. "What daughter?"

"There is way more to the story. Julie was pregnant when we

graduated from grade 12, just showing but as she was always a larger person no one noticed, and she hid it well."

"What?" I was her best friend. "How come she didn't tell me?"

"Well, she is very Catholic and having sex before marriage you know was forbidden and getting pregnant is an even bigger no, no. Her mom sent her away to stay with her aunt, who was a nun in a convent. When Julie had the baby, she gave it up for adoption. I guess Jim knew she was pregnant but did not want to marry Julie, so she had no choice." explained Marg.

"In order to save face and their good name she gave the baby away and never spoke of it again. Both went on with their lives and married different people." Vivian replied.

"The reunion brought back old memories and feelings, so they hooked up, divorced their current partners and married and are now looking for their little girl. She would not be so little now but maybe close to 40 years old."

"Are you kidding me? Just like that." I shouted.

"Yes, just like that." They both interjected.

"Wow, are you sure you are not fibbing me."

"No way would I lie." cried Marg.

"That sounds like a soap to me. Are you sure? You did not read this in a book or watch it on The Edge of Night." I remarked.

Story 2
Accident

"Where is Jimmy?"

"I don't know."

"What do you mean? Did you not leave today to go out hunting for geese?" Mom replied.

"Yes, but we never caught anything, so we came home."

"Well, where he is now?"

"He went home." I said hastily.

"His dad just phoned and says he is not home, and it is eight pm already and a school night. Where did he go?"

"He said he was going home."

"What happened to him?" mom pestered.

"Why are you asking all these questions? He went home and I came home about six pm in time for supper. No luck. We did not shoot a duck and that is it," I said angrily.

"Where is the gun?" Mom interjected.

"I don't know. Jimmy had it and he took the last shot and missed."

"Really?" mom questioned.

The cops were called. Jimmy was never found.

Until now... 30 years later.

"They found a body by the slough. It is heavily decomposed, and they are doing DNA testing to see if it could be Jimmy," said the police officer.

"I thought he ran away from home as he did not want to get a strap for not doing his chores and failing at school. His report card was thrown away," I said smartly.

"Bob, your sister is a nurse. She says if one does not deal with the past the past deals with you. Bob, you need to tell us what really happened that day on the pond?" said the policewoman.

I lit up another joint and tried to block out the memories of the past. Jimmy would be 45 now like me. We were best friends. The marijuana helped momentarily, the pills, alcohol, I needed it all to deal with my pain. I was a drug addict.

"What really happened?" Mike, my brother asked.

"It was an accident. He was my best friend, and we were shooting at some ducks. Jimmy started running towards the slough. But I did not see him. I thought he was a duck and like that he was gone."

"Jimmy," I cried, "Jimmy, please Jimmy come back. Please do not do this to me. I love you man."

I held and tenderly cradled him. I was so scared and did not know what to do so I just covered him up by the pond," I sobbed loudly.

Bob had his share of problems as he put out his joint and entered the Dube Centre for Mental Health and Addiction.

666-Conn

Before Internet or online dating during the 1990's people placed ads in the personal column, to meet and date people. As I did not go to bars; they were known as meat markets then, I thought I would give it a try.

I answered an ad which said:

"Male age 40, semi-retired driver, living on acreage near Saskatoon, Saskatchewan hobbies auto restoration, built 130 show cars, would rather play on the floor with his grandkids them watch TV."

Wow! Sounds like a keeper to me. And not bad looking.

His ad should have said: Phone 666-conn!

Clue Number 1 – Meeting at 9:30 am. on normal workday week, a Tuesday, when other people were at work. I was at the university, finishing my master thesis.

Clue Number 2 – Drove a beat up, rusty old Chevy truck and dealt in cars.

Clue Number 3 – Truck filled with junk, not cleaned out, cowboy boots still in truck from trip two weeks ago.

Clue Number 4 – After one hour of coffee, still wanted to stay with me all day. Checked his list and said there were five things on it and none of them were urgent. He could waste the day with me. I thought it was a compliment that he would spend the day with me. I did not know he had nothing else in his life. No real ambition and did not like to work.

Fact Number 1 – I was conned.

Fact Number 2 – I was scammed.

Fact Number 3 – I was taken advantage of.

Fact Number 4 – I was lied to.

Sounds stupid as I am writing. There are many dishonest people that conn people in relationships, not just in business deals. Why I am writing this? So other people might become aware of the signs.

I was innocent and young and did not know how to "play the field" and was too trustworthy. If someone told me, they were semi-retired I would think they were retired from another job and had a pensionable income so could afford to work part-time.

Another day, another set of clues:

Clue Number 1 – Driving to Edmonton, Alberta the truck stalled on the side of the road, not out of gas but out of oil; he is an auto mechanic.

Clue Number 2 – The muffler was held on by a wire.

Fact Number 1 – Old beater truck.

Fact Number 2 – Run out of oil, really.

Fact Number 1 – Boy, am I not thinking.

Fact Number 2 – Boy, am I dumb.

Fact Number 3 – Boy, am I stupid – hello!

Another day, another chance to clue in:

Go for lunch with his elderly parents.

Clue Number 1 – I suggest to him we pay for lunch.

Clue Number 2 – I suggest again we pick up the tab to buy his parent's lunch.

Clue Number 3 – I pay the bill as he had no money with him.

Fact Number 1 – I should not have to suggest he pay the bill he should just take it and pay.

Fact Number 2 – These are his parents, and I am suggesting he buy his parents' lunch.

Fact Number 3- Semi-retired and he has no money with him.

I should have said, "Three strikes and you are out"

Ok this gets better.

We took a pre-marriage weekend course to see if we are compatible and should get married. During the course we completed a survey of questions.

Clue Number 1 – Many incompatible areas noted.

Clue Number 2 – The marriage counselor suggests we hold off on the wedding till these areas are worked out.

Clue Number 3 – She suggests there are huge problems on the rating scale, and we might not want to get married at this time.

Fact Number 1 – I agree with her and point this out to him.

Fact Number 2 – He says he does not see the problem; it is only a rating scale and we can work those things out.

Fact Number 3 – He says is madly in love with me and those little things can be worked out. He will change them.

If someone wants to con you, they have an answer for everything. They are very convincing, have a plan or agenda and are very powerful at persuasion. They isolate you from family, get you alone and spend every minute with you so as not to give you an opportunity to talk to other people or think for yourself. All techniques that work very well for brainwashing strategies. The Saskatoon Star Phoenix paper says one third of people are scammed in some way.

I did not see the signs. But in hindsight, I do not think he allowed me to see the signs. He had an excuse or reason for everything and even when I tried to talk about it, he would change the topic or assure me everything would be alright. He swept me off my feet and come on now girls, who doesn't like being swept off their feet?

He would make music tapes of my favourite songs, all love songs like "Keeper of the Stars."

"It was no accident me finding you someone had a hand in it long before we ever knew or I could love you like that." by Joe Diffy or Randy Travis, "I'm going to love you forever and ever, Amen!"

Fact Number 1 – Half-truths are lies in disguise.

Fact Number 2 – Never believe everything he tells you even if you have been with the guy for years and he tells you what you want to hear.

Fact Number 3 – The best salesperson or con man can get you no matter what you do if they have their sights on you. It is like being assaulted. They will do whatever it takes to get what they want from you. In my case, it was marriage so I could financial support his semi-retired state. He was living on welfare on a $35,000 dollar acreage bought and owned by his parents. He said he built show cars, but rarely tinkered on a car and could not put in a motor.

So, what happened?

Two major things:

He threw the remote through the TV to demonstrate how much he loved me. He said the TV was not important to him and he loved me more than any TV. The second was that he could not hold down a job. In 10 years, he couldn't keep a single job. When fired, of course, he blamed the boss.

In the story of Bambi when the skunk was "Twitter pated" he could not function as he was so much in love. Please note that is a bad sign. When someone is that much in love, perhaps it is not love at all.

The world has some sketchy people.

I do not feel bad now, as Dr. Phil says, "People who conn the innocent, know what they are doing, play on your emotions, and are trained liars. It is not completely your fault. Life is a game to them as they are truly conns."

Beware of Number 666-CONN

Wrangled

The email said, "Send in your resumé if interested in volunteering for the CBC award show for the CCMA." Saskatchewan was known as the volunteer capital of Canada and Saskatoon was hosting the Canadian Country Music Awards for the first time, even though Vic Dubois had tried to bring it to Saskatoon for the past 22 years. The time had come, and Saskatoon was hosting.

Why would I not send in my resumé for a volunteer request like that? Sounds like fun, I thought.

The next day I tried to get into my Hotmail to find out if I was selected and my password did not work. I was hacked. Oh sh**... not now... what am I going to do? How I am going to find out if I get to work with the talent?

That is what the email said when I sent in my resumé. They were looking for people to work with the talent. I phoned my sister and my girlfriend and said that I might be working with the talent. Wow, would I really get to work with the country and western award stars? No way, I thought, no, I better not get my hopes up and get crushed. The talent... What does that mean exactly? I guess I will have to wait and see.

Oh crap! How am I to find that out? I can't get into my Hotmail. I've been hacked.

Desperately, I tried to get my password back and my Hotmail account working, but it said no access. I was locked out. It did not work.

What was I to do?

I had already signed up to volunteer to work at the cabaret Friday night at Prairie Land with all the western bands playing like Emerson and Doc Walker. 3,500 people were coming to a sold-out cabaret. I was to work as a ticket taker. Ok, fine but I really wanted to work with the talent.

Tuesday night, a volunteer launch party was held at the Pat in downtown Saskatoon, a volunteer orientation party. My friend, Margaret and I picked up our vests. Brad Johner played and another great band called "Thunder Rose."

They were fantastic. I would have loved to do the two-step to that band. Unfortunately, no partners. Oh well, a bunch of us ladies hit the dance floor and boogied in a circle. Hey, when you love to dance... you just dance, even if it is in a circle with girlfriends.

After the dance party, I headed home. Was I surprised at the voice mail on my answering machine? A man from CBC called, let's just call him George.

The message: Can you please phone me at this number and confirm that you will be a wrangler at the CBC awards show on Sunday?

What the heck is a wrangler, I thought?

It was late about midnight and I knew Toronto was two hours ahead.

Better not phone now and confirm as it was two am. I did not want to wake anyone and piss them off.

I will phone first thing in the morning.

Should I or should I not phone? Little did I know that these producers rarely sleep and pull all niters all the time to keep the show going. Thursday, I head off to Credit Union Centre to meet the team and get wrangled. Is it what I think it is? Really...

When we meet the team, one of the first things the leader has us do is sign a disclosure saying we will not disclose information about our guests. Can you do that?

Later after orientation and training. The big moment occurred, and George handed out the logistics package for the country star you get to wrangle or oversee for the next three days. Yes, the same George that left the message on my voicemail. He handed out the sheets for around 100 people. The job was exactly what I thought. We got to be the right-hand person, meet and greet and talk with the talent, the big stars.

First, I was told I was wrangler for the big kahuna, then suddenly George switches and I got... Yes, really it was in my hands for five minutes I was going to be a wrangler for the big one, oh no... too good to be true... for five minutes I was going to be a wrangler for him... Wow!

There were about 50 wranglers in the room.

Susan says, "Is there anyone that cannot be here Friday and Saturday? I need to know now."

I thought when we signed up, we had to be available all three days. What do you mean?

This one girl puts up her hand. "I can only be here Sunday."

George, dear, sweet gentle, George came up to me and took my logistics package from my hand and said, "May I?"

May I? May I??? So politely... I said, "No George, not him? I saw him in concert. He's awesome. I love him."

It was gone. His logistics package was taken from my hands and given to the girl who could only be here Sunday. Whaaaaa!

George brought me another package, oh well, say a prayer. I will just go with the flow; this guy is not too shabby either. He is still a great star. I'm just gonna have fun and try my best to be the best wrangler.

So, what does a wrangler do?

Our job was to take care of the stars and make sure they have what they need, and know where they are, when they are supposed to be on stage and get them on time for their makeup, hair, dress rehearsal. I was on call for that person for the next three days. I got to meet, talk, but no hounding, no pictures, no autographs.

"Be professional, were the instructions and make sure you know where your star is at all times. Do not lose them. Whatever you do, do not lose your star. You need to know where they are at all times."

Wrangling was what I thought and more. What an experience! What fun! What joy! What happened next? The weekend of a lifetime. The best damn experience ever, the most fun and a bucket list dream I could not have imagined. Who would have thought, a small town, Saskatchewan girl would get to be a wrangler?

I knew I had hit the big time when I was a wrangler. This was more than any triple A bucket list experience. We always wore walkie-talkies and got directions from the CBC top brass producers. My three days of fun began when my walkie-talkie directed me to loading dock number four to pick up my star's band.

When I met the bus and the band, I said, "Hi, I'm your wrangler for the next three days."

The bus driver smiled and said, "Hop in, I will give you a ride to the other docket."

And when my star's agent says to me, "Do you have any gum?" I said, "Sure, and then said, "keep the package." He said, "You're the best wrangler, we've ever had. You are professional, friendly and fun." My face lit up like a star. I knew I was in for the ride of a lifetime. I met the entire band and of course, the big man himself and his agent and his press agent and his team and they were so nice and so wonderful and my, my, my, wow was all I can say. Thank you for the wonderful wrangling opportunity, pick me, anytime to be a wrangler.

The Deep Sleep

Preamble...

Once upon a time, long ago, when humans lived in caves; it was safe at night. Well, almost safe. When the sun went down, when darkness covered the earth, the biggest predators for humans were nature, weather and animals.

Fire changed all that. Humans now had protection from the cold and animals, day and night. Darkness prevailed until... Eureka! Thomas Edison invented the light bulb.

The earth, humans, were never the same. With the invention of the light bulb, sleep disorders arose in catastrophic numbers. People could stay up all night with the magic light bulb. They could work all night too. They were now in control of their lives 24/7 or so they thought. But were they really in charge? And who would protect them – especially the women?

Enter the 21st century and the New Government Order. (N.G.O.)

Year: 2050

Planet: Earth

Humans vs. Humans

Hassle-free sleep brought to you by your sponsors N.G.O.

The government can help you oversee your destiny.

We interrupt this TV show with this important news bulletin.

First Alert: All humans must attend their first safety clinic to pick up their sleep key.

Epidemic warning: Do you have sleep problems? Do you have a sleep phobia? Are you afraid to fall asleep at night? Lack of sleep is epidemic on Earth.

N.G.O. is here to help you solve your sleep problem.

Urgent: Tap your left wrist implant to download your APP and lock into channel zzz's.

Remember: Lack of sleep causes drowsiness, accidents, mental fatigue, weight problems, overeating, forgetfulness, relationship breakdowns and even death.

Lock into Station zzz's to pick your sleep package.

Lock into #1 for Uninterrupted Sleep

Lock into #2 for Pleasant Dreams

Lock into #3 for Erotic Dreams

Lock into #4 for Career Training (how to become a teacher, a lawyer – you pick a career)

Lock into #5 for Business Online Training

Lock into #6 for Memory Training

Lock into #7 for Sleep Training for new mothers with babies

Lock into #8 for Exercise Training

Lock into #9 for Mind Training

Lock into #10 for Retraining the Criminal Mind

Lock into #11 for women only

Lock into #12 for help with overcoming feelings as a failed mother

Lock into #13 for help with a loss of identity as a female in the androgynous future

Lock into #14 for getting out of abusive relationships

Simple instructions, simple downloads, simplify your sleep.

N.G.O. is here for you. And for women in emergency

situations, a special hidden app operated by your estrogen levels automatically gives a direct line to Natalia.

Simply pick up your key, set your password, program your chip or download a sleep APP right into your spinal port. You pick. Plug in your port, your bed, your memory chip, your key and enjoy the full benefits of your chosen sleep package.

Society benefits from your choices, sleep packages, additional training when you sleep.

So, close your eyes and fall asleep and dream your life back to good health.

This commercial is a paid advertisement and brought to you from:

The New Government Order (N.G.O.)

Two Point Five Hours

It was not a whole day. Two point five hours out of twenty-four. 150 minutes. 9,000 seconds. That's all it was. What if it was the last two point five hours of your life?

I thought, what the hell. If she could climb this, I could do it. I am a trained professional, she isn't.

I had never climbed anything so high; 60 metres above a construction pit with rebar jutting out like spikes, a construction crane with slanted steel beams. I had never climbed such a barrier before even during the multitude of training exercises with the Toronto firefighters. I was a woman and felt that this woman was in trouble. I wanted to rescue her. Woman to woman! It was an act of love.

After a lot of convincing, my Captain finally agreed to let me climb this structure. I finally convinced him by reminding him that along with my training I had been a trained arborist working with ropes in trees. Right, what was I thinking? I should have let Charlie do it!

It looked daunting. Yet, she had done it in black boots with heels in a blue jean jacket and it was cold. The higher you got the colder. How long did it take her to master this crane? She had climbed 60 metres to the top and slid 15 metres down a greasy cable to land on the hook. And there she sat swaying in the breeze.

What was she doing up there? How long had she been up

there? All kinds of questions generated in my mind as I ascended my climb to heaven. Or was it possibly hell? Depends on my belief and the outcome. What was my belief? I wondered.

Each step would bring me closer to the answer, the truth. But I knew when I reached her it was not mine to ask. It was none of my business. I just needed to get to her safely. All I needed to do was bring her down.

How many steps would it be? I calculated. The crane is how high? My rescue supplies included multiple cables and ropes, and weighed how much? Lots to think about as I climbed.

Slowly, I made my way to the top, no room for slipping. There were times in the first hour I counted the steps. Then the next 20 minutes, I questioned my sanity, then my physical needs began to kick in. Bathroom, I did not want to drink water as where would I pee? Practical needs. Hunger, not really. I was a bundle of nerves. That slowed hunger cravings. However, the more I climbed, exerted energy, exhaustion began creeping into my muscles and joints. Hell, I was 53 years old.

I kept thinking of my family, my husband, my two children. Would my husband ever see me again, alive? Would I be able to hold him again? Make love to him? Would I be able to see my children grow up? Graduate school, talk to them and kiss and tuck them in at night? What was I doing volunteering for this job? I must be nuts! All I knew is a woman needed my help.

The mind works overtime during stress and yes, it plays trick on you. Hand over hand. Keep your feet moving. Don't stop. Keep going, one minute, you feel crazy, the next second, ok stop now, back and forth like the pendulum in my Grandpa's clock. I was playing an entire tournament in my mind and body. Was I winning? The clock was ticking. Tick, tock.

Finally, the top, it was so cold my nose started to run and again my physical needs took over. Bathroom, food, water, warmth played in my mind. Over and over – what am I doing here?

When I get down, I am so soaking in a hot jacuzzi tub, with candles and the whole nine yards. When I get down, I am sleeping for 24 hours straight. When I get down, I am having a stiff drink – a scotch on the rocks – make it a double.

The descent to reach the girl was gruelling. I needed to get from the top of the crane, down the cable without landing on her causing her to fall. I needed to attach the hook to the girl without her toppling off. This is where the expertise of my crew, damn good luck and lots of prayers are needed. The sweat was dripping from my forehead as we made eye contact.

"I have a pickle-ball game, playing at eight fifteen tonight. Have you ever played pickleball? It is like ping-pong only played with a whiffle ball and paddle on a court instead of a table. It is the fastest growing sport in North America." I rambled on.

I was talking to keep her calm, but she appeared calmer than me and was worried about getting in trouble. I reassured her I would help pay her fine with my Tim Horton's cards. Humour helps relax the troubled beast. Fire personnel get lots of gifted Tim Horton's cards like teachers.

The descent, a crew member used a mechanized system to lower me on the ropes. There on the crane, was a lovely young lady of about 20 something. What does one say when you meet someone for the first time after dangling like dental thread on a ledge?

"Hey, how's it going?" I ask hesitantly. There she was sitting on a plank atop a hook 45 metres above a construction pit. She was calm and cool as a cucumber or so it seemed. Me, I was scared shitless.

Was she suicidal? What brought her to the top of that

towering crane? A broken relationship? A pregnancy? A rape? Women have to deal with so many issues these days. Life can be overwhelming.

Again, thoughts raced through my mind like a marathon of long distant runners.

"I am Samantha, but you can call me Sam. Can I put this rescue harness on you?"

We talked about the beautiful picturesque view and the need for a camera. Anything to take our mind off the problem at hand, getting her down safely, not her real problems. Why was she here in the first place?

She seemed relieved I was there, another woman and said sure, "I want to come down."

I fastened her in carefully and together we were brought down, we clung to each other in "a death grip" the descent might seem long, only 30 minutes, but compared to the two-hour ascent was like a jaunt, a lot quicker than the climb. She felt like an ice cube. Her jeans, and light jean jacket was not enough to keep her warm. I was tempted to ask her why as the crane was lowered, but professionally I could not. The woman in me, the mother in me, wanted to talk to her, console her, hug her and cry with her, to help relieve her pain.

I just said words of comfort. "I am glad you are ok. I am here to help you."

Things I was trained to say as a rescue worker, but I meant it, truly in my heart.

The crowd that had formed and watched the entire two point five hours, 150 minutes, 90,000 seconds were still there. Cheering me on clapping, madly.

"That lady should be given the key to the city," said an observer.

The media in a frenzy, trying to tell the story. My story, our story.

I said to her, "I don't even know your name."

She said, "Marisa. My boyfriend dumped me, and I am pregnant, and I feel hopeless and stupid and I don't know why I did such a stupid thing."

"Don't worry you are in good hands now. No man is worth ending your life. There are women's groups with excellent professional counselling to help you deal with all of this. Just ask!"

Rescue workers took her, but before they did, I gave her a huge hug and said, "You are a special person and don't forget it. Us women, have to help each other out and stick together. That is why I volunteered to rescue you."

Then they handcuffed and put her in an ambulance to take her to the hospital to be checked up and charged. Six counts of mischief. What she did was illegal. I wanted to ask her, find out, how she did it, climbed so high in her two-inch, high-heeled boots without cables and ropes, so we could train other firefighters. The professional in me coming out.

And me... what did I do after the parade of reporters and pictures.

I called my husband on my cell and said, "Honey, I really love you. Where are the kids?"

(Short story based on CBC News Toronto report: from the web and the Saskatoon Star Phoenix: Thursday, April 27th, 2017-NP2)

Live Well

Prelude:

Age is just a number or is it? Many people are living to 100 today and are in great shape, doing remarkable things. On a science show I once saw, it said, someone born this year has the capability to live to 150. I have two friends that want to live to 100. One is 94 and she exclaimed the last time I saw her, that unfortunately that is only six years away. The other person is 72 years-old and almost in his last quarter of a century. Maybe, one day I will write a book on advice to live to 100.

For now, I feel content with what I have and who I have become. I feel blessed and grateful for everyday God has given me and try not to think about how long I will live. More importantly, I appreciate life, try and enjoy it and be kind. A simple philosophy.

As the story goes… Live well and be kind.

I hope my three greatest treasures, Symret, Natasha and Jacob-Joshua will understand and be grateful for their wonderful gift of life. I have had an enjoyable career as a teacher (30 years) and now a remarkably interesting life as an author. (15 books and counting). I always say "Want to change your life? Write a book."

Life is never easy. I am happy to have had all the lessons that hopefully has made me a better person and try to create a better world. I feel I am a compassionate listener, and people watcher. People are drawn to me and tell me things I do not even want to know. A friend said if something bad happens in your life, think of it as good writing material.

Writing is my therapy. Are these stories real or fictional? Some are and some aren't. You have the privilege of figuring that out. Creative fiction and nonfiction are wonderful genres.

"Live well!" is what she said. Mary MacIsaac was 108 years-old and living in Saskatoon, Saskatchewan. (now deceased) She was Saskatchewan's oldest living centenarian in the year 2000 and the second oldest person alive in Canada.

Her motto can be broken down into five points:

1 – "The only thing that matters in life is what you do for others."
2 – "People are more tolerant than they used to be. There is less anti-religious feeling and understanding has grown."
3 – "I couldn't live without my faith – I couldn't think about it…"
4 – "Cracked wheat porridge, one soft-boiled egg and a cup of hot water is my breakfast every day of my life."
5 – "When I wake up, I always look forward to a new day."

These are a few beliefs, feelings, and her wonderful words of wisdom for aging.

Now deceased, I still remember the pleasure of our meeting and her interview. I had interviewed 13 centenarians in the year 2000 for a video documentary I worked on called, "Goatsmilk, Sauerkraut and Prayer."

It was created to honour and recognize those Saskatchewan seniors who had lived in three different centuries, nineteenth, twentieth and twenty- first. The Saskatchewan Government deemed them, "The Three Century Club" recognizing 179 members living in Saskatchewan in the year 2000 and then held a tea in their honour in Regina, SK. and created a plaque with their names on it.

For me, I tried to find out the secret to their longevity. I created video interviews put together with help of the video department at the University of Saskatchewan.

"Live well!" Mary's words seemed too simple a philosophy.

What does it mean?

I was hoping for a magic potion or pill that created their lives of longevity. Those 13 individuals amazed me and were in a remarkable mental state. The common thread was a unique spiritual dimension that reached even to the one man that professed atheism. His philosophy was "love your neighbour as yourself."

Perhaps that is the key and common denominator I found in my quest for longevity.

Over the years I have had time to ponder those interviews. One of the most important ideas that I noted was that the individuals interviewed kept active or wanted to keep active. For example, Dewy Pinder, at 102 years-old and living in Melville, SK. still wanted to go horseback riding and dance at his great granddaughter's wedding.

Dewy espoused that; "Farmers should quit using chemicals and take care of the earth."

"We may be here for a long time."

"The greatest thing, you'll ever learn, is just to love, and be loved in return!"

Dewey continued by saying:

"The golden years, as promised by commercials, do not seem all that golden for some people. It seems as people age, many live with great regret for events in the past, which sometimes causes depression or sometimes they live in the future which causes great worry or anxiety. I try and stay in the present moment and live "one day at a time" just like that old spiritual hymn "one day at time, sweet Jesus."

Spiritual just like the centenarians.

I have a girlfriend, who has a zest for living. Eileen is ninety-four years-old and wants to live till 100. When I told her that a science program suggested that someone born this year, in 2020 could live to 150 years old. She said without hesitation or a blink, "I volunteer!"

Wow!

"My biggest fear" says Dewey upon aging, "is being inactive or unable to dance. I love to walk every day. I do not want to be in a wheelchair or unable to move."

However, it seems many seniors besides coping with dementia have mental health issues. Some seem to have lost reason and sanity and are into a lot of drama, becoming like kids again, losing tempers, fighting with their peers or just terribly angry. 63 years of living, a lifelong learner, perhaps does not qualify me to comment on aging, as there are a great many elderly now living to 100 years and in great shape physically and mentally.

However, observation is a powerful tool and as a writer I observe a lot. I find "loving" and "living simply" in a complicated, materialistic culture is an easier way to live.

"Live well" makes more sense. If one "lives well" they have no regrets and do not hate the past or worry about tomorrow. That is how I have decided to live and if Mary's philosophy doesn't work just "being kind" might help create a few golden years and some special memories. I choose simple living and showing great kindness as my way of life.

*Lilac Bush
at the Nisbit Provincial Forest, Saskatchewan
by Macdowall.*

Constant Craving in the Year of COVID-19

Pandemic! What did I know about that?

After three months in lock down, I realized I hate puzzles. At least I listened to my old CD'S during my puzzle making. Yes, they still make CDs. Singing along with my favourite old tunes; that helped keep my sanity.

One would think that a lock down would be perfect for a writer. Isolation, staying inside, no one around to bug you. Sure, isolation is like going on a diet. I rarely eat chocolate – do not have a big, sweet tooth. I prefer salty foods like popcorn and chips.

However, if I decide to go on a diet today – guess what? Give me chocolate and ice cream and everything I do not normally crave. I want to eat it all.

"Constant Craving," so says k.d.lang. This pandemic is like that. Things you might not normally do, you want to do.

Yes, "People are Strange" says the American Rock band, The Doors. Covid-19 has brought out the worst in some people. Yet, to those front-line workers it has brought out the best. I thank you.

Life is full of lessons and Covid-19 for me reinforced the idea that one does not need a lot of material possessions to survive. Shelter, food, clothing. This was a good time to save money except for the Amazon spenders.

One could save for future travel, on shows, on food by cooking and not eating at restaurants and save on fees for the extra things like gyms. It is a time to promote family values and spend time together. Covid-19 is an opportunity to play all the board games bought, build up relationships and have family time. If your family was around.

Time – our most precious commodity. How do you spend it? My mom, Sophie taught us to create our own fun. This Covid-19 Time is the perfect time to learn a craft, write a song, learn to play an instrument or simply enjoy some me time.

We are all different people having experienced and survived our first world Covid-19 pandemic. Living with masks is only a small sacrifice, once you wrap your head around the fact that you are saving your life and someone else's too.

Cocooning, as a single woman was hard as I went from a very active calendar as an author and singer performing at nursing homes as The Sassy Sisters with my sister Angie and book readings at schools to an empty classroom, in one day.

Old Barn in Saskatchewan

It was a shocker, dealing with the joy of being alone and the heart break of not seeing my family. Going to the store to buy toilet paper and there was none available, in my opinion, is a first world problem. I grew up on a farm with no running water and no indoor plumbing. Some might be surprised that we used the Eaton's catalogue for toilet paper. I was afraid that I might have to revert back to those days.

I even started making my own cards to send to people, wrote some letters and snail mailed them. And for an author, well, it became writing time once you figured out that Covid-19 was not going away anytime soon. Learning to live with Covid-19 is the new normal.

This happened to the Women Suffragists and they never gave up. For example: during the Spanish flu, which arrived in 1918,

My Grandparent's Old Farmhouse
3 kilometres west and six kilometers north of Hafford, Saskatchewan.

it complicated plans for Suffragists as illness was everywhere, gatherings were banned, and plans cancelled. Sound familiar? Yet, women prevailed, survived and got the vote. We will also prevail, in spite of what is happening in the world. Continue your good will and your good work.

The reality is, once someone says you can't do something or go out all you think about is travelling to Cuba, going to a movie, playing pickleball. A game like Ping-Pong but played on a court.

Life continues to teach us daily lessons. Our human spirit is resilient and can survive if we start taking care of each other. All of my prairie family instincts of love and generosity start to kick in.

I wrote a poetry book during my 6-month Covid-19 lockdown called: Race to Finish. If Covid-19 doesn't kill us and if humans do not smarten up as a race, stop systemic racism and don't stop killing each other we will destroy this world and each other. People need to recognize injustices and that Black and Indigenous Lives Matter! Can we race to finish? Together.

As a woman, a mother, a teacher, a human being we can make a difference in the world. So, let's do it. Live well through Covid-19. This is our test for the future. More importantly, "Live Well" everyday and be kind. And stop racism!

About the Author

Marion Mutala has a master's degree in educational administration and taught for 30 years. Passionate for the arts, she loves to write, read, sing, play guitar and pickleball and travel. Marion's National Award-Winning bestseller, Baba's Babushka: A Magical Ukrainian Christmas (Anna Pidrucheny Award), was published in 2010. Other titles from that series are Baba's Babushka: A Magical Ukrainian Easter (Nominated for a Sask. Book Award 2013) and Baba's Babushka: A Magical Ukrainian

Wedding, (International High Plains Book Award for Best Children's book-2014). Marion released Grateful in 2014, followed with The Time for Peace is Now, and released a debut book of poetry, Ukrainian Daughter's Dance in 2016. Her first murder mystery called, The Mechanic's Wife (winner of Destiny Publishing Contest) was released in 2016 as well as another children's book called, More Babas, Please! in 2017. Kohkom's Babushka: A Magical Metis/Ukrainian Tale was released 2017 and My Buddy, Dido! (Nominated for High Plains Book Award 2019) was released 2018. Her first young adult book called, My Dearest Dido, The Holodomor Story – a powerful book about the Ukrainian genocide, the Holodomor was just released in 2019. Just released in 2020, a chapbook by Happy Leopard Press called Earth Angels: Operation Angel with all profits going to Nashi a Ukrainian organization that tries to stop human trafficking. Also released in 2020 as a 10th year anniversary hardcover collection of her four Baba's Books called Baba's Babushka: Magical Ukrainian Adventures with a new book included called Baba's Babushka: A Magical Ukrainian Journey. Coming soon: a poetry book called Race to Finish.

Visit www.babasbabushka.ca to learn more about Marion's work.